THIRTEEN DAYS/ NINETY MILES

THIRTEEN DAYS/ NINETY MILES:

THE CUBAN MISSILE CRISIS

NORMAN H. FINKELSTEIN

JULIAN (M) MESSNER
Published by Simon & Schuster
New York   London   Toronto   Sydney   Tokyo   Singapore

JULIAN Ⓜ MESSNER
Published by Simon & Schuster
1230 Avenue of the Americas
New York, New York 10020

Manufactured in the United States of America

1   3   5   7   9   10   8   6   4   2

Library of Congress Cataloging-in-Publication Data

Finkelstein, Norman H.
    Thirteen days/ninety miles : the Cuban missile crisis.
        p.   cm.
    Includes bibliographical references and index.
    1. Cuban Missile Crisis, 1962. [1. Cuban Missile Crisis, 1962.]
    I. Title.   II. Title: 13 days/90 miles.
    E841.F48 1994 973.922—dc20 93–29425 CIP AC
                ISBN 0–671–86622–2

For Jenn and Jeff

CONTENTS

ACKNOWLEDGMENTS

I wish to acknowledge the cheerful and competent assistance of the professional staff at the John F. Kennedy Presidential Library in Boston. In particular, I am indebted to archivists June Payne, Maura Porter, Ronald Whealan, Jim Cedrone, Alan Goodrich, and Donna Cotterell.

Much of the current knowledge of the Cuban Missile Crisis results from the persistence of scholars at the National Security Archives, a private organization. Through their use of the Freedom of Information Act, a 1966 law that allows access to federal government documents, previously restricted files have been declassified. These newly available documents permit historians and students of history to learn more about important events.

Many of the direct quotations in this book are from documents and meeting transcripts located in the files of the John F. Kennedy Library or reproduced by the National Security Archives in its book, *The Cuban Missile Crisis, 1962*.

Much of the research for this book was conducted under a Fellowship for Independent Study awarded by the Council for Basic Education and the National Endowment for the Humanities.

I am especially grateful to Dr. Michael Kort of Boston University for his meticulous review and critique of this manuscript. Finally, I thank my wife, Rosalind, for her continued understanding, patience, and keen editorial eye.

Little, Brown and Company for quotations from

Khrushchev Remembers, The Glasnost Tapes by
    Nikita Khrushchev,
copyright 1990 by Little, Brown and Company.
Translation copyright 1990, Jerrold L. Schecter.

Macmillan Publishing Company for quotations from

John F. Kennedy, President by Hugh Sidey,
copyright 1963 by Hugh Sidey.

The Kennedy Legacy by Theodore C. Sorensen,
copyright 1969 by Theodore C. Sorensen.

Khrushchev and the First Russian Spring by
    Fedor Burlatsky,
copyright 1988 by Fedor Burlatsky.
Translated from the Russian by Daphne Skillen,
English translation copyright 1991, Daphne Skillen.
A Robert Stewart Book, reprinted by permission of
    Charles Scribner's Sons, an imprint of Macmillan
    Publishing Company.

Roy A. Medvedev for quotations from

Khrushchev, A Biography by Roy A. Medvedev,
copyright 1983 by Roy A. Medvedev.
Published by Doubleday and Company.

The New Press for quotations from

The Cuban Missile Crisis, 1962 edited by
    Lawrence Chang and Peter Kornbluh,
copyright 1992 by Lawrence Chang and
    Peter Kornbluh.

W. W. Norton and Company, Inc., for quotations from

Thirteen Days by Robert F. Kennedy,
copyright 1969 by W. W. Norton and Company.

Random House, Inc., for quotations from

Danger and Survival by McGeorge Bundy,
copyright 1988 by McGeorge Bundy.

Eyeball to Eyeball by Dino A. Brugioni,
copyright 1991 by Dino A. Brugioni.

War and Peace in the Nuclear Age by John Newhouse,
copyright 1988 by John Newhouse and WGBH Educational Foundation.

Photo acknowledgments:

pages 16, 17, 20, 29, 33, 39, 41, 46, 48, 49, 54, 55, 60, 63, 65, 67, 71, 74, 84, 93, 99, 102, 106: The John F. Kennedy Library.

page 22: The National Archives.

ONE

THE COLD WAR HEATS UP

❖ ❖ ❖

*"Aggressive conduct, if allowed to grow unchecked and
unchallenged, ultimately leads to war."*
(JOHN F. KENNEDY)

The United States and the Soviet Union never directly went to war against each other. Indeed, during World War II both fought on the same side against Nazi Germany. When the war ended, the two countries resumed their previously intense rivalry in a "cold war" that lasted until the fall of the Soviet Union in 1990. For over four decades both countries faced each other with nuclear weapons in a nervous state of neither war nor peace.

Since the time of its birth in the Communist Revolution of 1917, the Soviet Union had coexisted uneasily with the United States in a climate of mutual hostility. To Americans the teachings of Communism were as alien and unwelcome as the repression and violence associated with it. The United States did not formally recognize the new Communist government until 1933. To most Americans, Russia's Communist rulers seemed even more repressive than the Czars they replaced. What frightened the United States and the rest of the democratic world most about Russia's new political system was the long-standing threat of world revolution and domination first expressed by the father of

Soviet Communism, Vladimir Lenin, and continued by his successors, Joseph Stalin and Nikita Khrushchev.

Upon Lenin's death in 1924 Joseph Stalin consolidated power and led the Soviet Union through the dark days of World War II. He was ruthless in carrying out his political ambitions. Labor camps in remotest Siberia became the final stop for anyone even suspected of being critical of him or the well-entrenched Soviet regime. He died in 1953.

Toward the end of World War II Soviet troops freed the countries of Eastern Europe from Nazi control but remained behind to insure Communist governmental takeovers. In one massive sweep, Stalin asserted his domination over Eastern Europe. Once independent countries, such as Latvia, Lithuania, Estonia, Czechoslovakia, Hungary, Poland, Romania, and Yugoslavia, suddenly found the hated Nazis replaced by Communist dictatorships. These takeovers helped reinforce Western mistrust of the Soviets. In 1946 Winston Churchill, prime minister of Great Britain, coined a phrase that symbolized Soviet aggression in Eastern Europe when he said, "An iron curtain has descended across the Continent." For the duration of the cold war, reference to the "iron curtain" countries conjured up sinister images of joyless people living without freedom.

In February 1945, toward the end of the war, the Allied leaders—Franklin Roosevelt of the United States, Winston Churchill of Great Britain, and Joseph Stalin of the Soviet Union—met at Yalta, a resort on the Black Sea, to decide Europe's postwar future. At Yalta the leaders agreed to divide Germany into four zones, each to be occupied by one of the major Allied victors—the United States, the Soviet Union, France, and Great Britain. Berlin, the capital of Nazi Germany, located within the Eastern, or Soviet, zone, would itself be divided into four parts. In addition, the Allied leaders agreed to support free elections for those countries liberated from German occupation.

Although the Soviets agreed to the free elections, they never had any intention of honoring that commitment. To Joseph Stalin, the Soviet dictator, control over Poland and the other countries bordering the Soviet Union was essential to prevent a future invasion of his country. The Potsdam Conference in July 1945, held near Berlin in recently conquered Germany, was the last time the leaders met as allies. Since the Yalta meeting, five months earlier, Franklin Roosevelt had died. The United States was now represented by a new president, Harry Truman. Hinting at the cold war to come, major disagreements arose at Potsdam about the political realities of dividing defeated Germany and the obvious communizing of Eastern Europe by the Soviet Union.

Three main world power blocs formed in the late 1940s and early 1950s. A new decade began on a note of unease and hostility as a new world balance of power took shape. The first, composed mainly of the Western democracies, was led by the United States. The second, controlled by the Soviet Union, consisted mainly of its newly conquered Eastern European neighbors. A third bloc, consisting of smaller, newly independent countries, was neutral in the struggle between the other two blocs. The fact that the two major powers, the United States and the Soviet Union, possessed nuclear weapons capable of destroying each other and possibly the rest of the world added to the volatile situation.

After surrounding itself with Communist satellite nations in Eastern Europe, the Soviet Union seized every opportunity to export Communism to other countries around the world. To balance what it saw as a threat to democracy, the United States announced the Truman Doctrine in 1947. The goal of this doctrine was to contain Soviet encroachment. In 1948 the United States instituted the Marshall Plan to support the recovery of war-devastated Europe. In an address to Congress in 1947 Truman stated, "It must be the policy of the United States to support free peoples who are resisting subjugation by armed minorities or by outside pressures."

In standing up to the Soviets, President Truman sent massive military and economic aid to counter Communist pressures in such widespread places as Greece, Turkey, and Iran. In addition, the Marshall Plan provided billions of dollars in aid to help European democracies rebuild working economies and thereby limit the appeal of Communism.

Tough talk was the order of the day from one American president to the next. President Truman said, "There isn't any difference between the totalitarian Russian government and the Hitler government . . . they are all alike. They are police governments—police state governments." At his inauguration in 1953 Truman's successor, Dwight Eisenhower, painted the differences between the Soviets and the United States in black and white terms. "Forces of good and evil are massed and armed . . . Freedom is pitted against slavery, lightness against dark."

The first major incident of cold war hostilities took place in Berlin. In March 1948 the freely elected government of Czechoslovakia was overthrown and replaced with a Communist regime. The lack of response from the West encouraged further Soviet action. When the United States, Britain, and France decided to join together the German zones they controlled to form West Germany, the Soviets applied pressure on West Berlin, with the aim of forcing the Western democracies to leave Germany.

Since the city of Berlin was totally surrounded by Communist-controlled territory, the Soviets easily began a blockade of West Berlin and halted all land, sea, and rail access to the city. In a brave show of support of the besieged West Berliners, the United States and its allies instituted a massive airlift, which over the months of the crisis brought in two million tons of food, clothes, fuel, and other essentials. The Soviets finally reopened the roads to Berlin in 1949 when they realized that the United States would not back down. During most of the cold war, Berlin remained a flash point in Soviet and United States relations.

To continue with the containment policy toward the Soviet Union, the United States, Canada, and ten European allies joined together in 1949 to form NATO, the North Atlantic Treaty Organization.[1] By the terms of the organization, any attack by the Soviets on one NATO member would be considered an attack on them all. In 1955 the Soviets countered by forming the Warsaw Pact, an organization made up of those countries overrun by the Soviet Union after World War II.

The fierce competition between the two blocs took a frightening turn in 1949 when the Soviet Union joined the United States as a nuclear power. At first there was just one superpower, the United States. In the final days of World War II the United States dropped the world's first atomic bomb on the city of Hiroshima, thereby bringing the war with Japan to a quick end. For the next few years possession of the atomic bomb and its secret technology made the United States the world's unchallenged military and political leader. When the Soviet Union stunned the world in 1949 with the news that it too had the bomb, it automatically catapulted itself to superpower status alongside the United States. As the years passed, the quantity and power of the nuclear inventory on both sides grew to the point that each side alone could totally destroy all life on earth many times over.

The year 1949 was also memorable for another event. Communist revolutionaries in China, led by Mao Zedong, successfully overthrew the existing government. The Communist revolution in China and news of Soviet atomic capability sent shock waves through the United States. Many Americans could not accept the challenge to their exclusive superpower status. Their victory in World War II now seemed hollow. They also found it hard to understand how the Soviet Union, devastated by war, could have made such technological progress so quickly. Many thought the Soviets had received help from traitorous Western governmental officials. Indeed, espionage on both sides increased after the war. Anti-Communist feelings, which had always existed, mushroomed into paranoid fear and loathing of the Soviet Union and Communism.

In Congress the House Un-American Activities Committee (HUAC), which began operations in 1938, swung into high gear in 1947. Its mission was to root out suspected pro-Communist activities within government and important national industries. The State Department was a key target of those who saw a Communist plot in every diplomatic decision and every American diplomatic failure.

Alger Hiss was a State Department official who had taken part in the Yalta Conference. He was accused of being a spy for the Soviet Union, although doubts about his guilt lingered for decades.

He went to jail, his professional life ruined, solely on the claim of a *Time* magazine editor who claimed that he and Hiss were Communist party members in the 1930s. In 1992 a former Soviet general declared that Hiss was never a Soviet spy, but many were still not prepared to accept the word of a former Communist. During the years of the cold war, the Hiss case came to symbolize fear of Communist infiltration on one hand and irresponsible, reputation-destroying "witch-hunts" on the other.

That period's fear of Communism and the blind desire to eradicate it was epitomized by the Republican junior senator from Wisconsin, Joseph R. McCarthy. His irresponsible and wildly unproven charges of Communist infiltration held the country spellbound. He accused the Roosevelt and Truman administrations of "twenty years of treason." Even when Republican President Eisenhower assumed office, McCarthy continued the attack, accusing the American war hero of having Communist leanings.

The postwar hunt for Communist sympathizers was relentless. In 1950 Congress passed the McCarran Act—officially called the Internal Security Act—to broaden police powers against suspected traitors. Many of the country's largest police forces formed special Red Squads. Only with the televised Army-McCarthy hearings in 1954 did Senator McCarthy's popularity begin to drop as more people began to realize the flimsiness and irresponsibility of his charges.[2] Although the hysteria of the McCarthy era eventually subsided, anti-Communism continued as a permanent fixture of American life in the 1950s. The worst insult a politician could hurl at an opponent was to call him or her a "Pinko" or "Commie."

The cold war continued to flame up in the 1950s in places many Americans had never heard of. At the end of World War II, Korea, for many years a Japanese territory, was temporarily divided between the United States and the Soviet Union until stable self-government could be arranged. In 1950 communist-run North Korea invaded South Korea. President Truman viewed the invasion as yet another Soviet challenge and turned to the United Nations (UN) for support. He hoped a united effort by the world's new peace-keeping body would discourage the Communists from a larger war. In charge of the UN troops was World War II war hero General Douglas MacArthur. After brilliantly pushing the North Koreans back across their own border, he led his UN troops northward, with UN approval, to unify the country.

As the UN troops approached the Chinese border, the president became nervous about Chinese involvement in a wider war and prohibited American attacks across the Chinese border. When Chinese troops in great numbers crossed the Yalu River and surprised UN troops, Truman reacted cautiously. He did not allow MacArthur to attack Chinese positions across the Yalu. "We believe," the Joint Chiefs of Staff said, "that Korea is not the place to fight a major war." MacArthur held other views, stating that "there is no substitute for victory."[3] MacArthur was relieved from duty and called home by Truman. The war in Korea dragged on.

In the presidential campaign of 1952 Dwight Eisenhower promised "I shall go to Korea." With his election, as battles continued to rage, peace talks continued. Although no formal peace treaty was arranged, both sides agreed to cease the hostilities in 1953. The shooting stopped, but the prewar borders and mutual distrust remained.

The Eisenhower years saw the emergence of a new way of dealing with the Soviets. Eisenhower's secretary of state was John Foster Dulles, a religious man who did not accept the containment philosophy of the previous Truman administration. Dulles believed Communism was a great evil and had to be confronted with a "spiritual offensive." Dulles advised the president to take the offensive around the globe to thwart, and in some cases overthrow, pro-Communist or anti-Western governments. The cold war grew more frigid. In Iran in 1953 and Guatemala in 1954 the Central Intelligence Agency (CIA) helped topple governments considered unfriendly to the United States.

After the death of Joseph Stalin in 1953, power eventually gravitated to Nikita Khrushchev, an obscure Communist party official. With a new leader in charge Soviet attitudes toward the West began to change. While Khrushchev attempted to soften Stalin's harsh dictatorial style, his desire was to equal the United States

militarily and economically. In foreign affairs however, some
things did not change. Any attempt by Soviet-dominated countries
to break away from Moscow's control was dealt with ruthlessly. The
harshness of these actions inflamed tensions between the superpowers. In the view of the United States the Soviet Union could
never be trusted. This lack of trust further escalated tensions between the two countries.

Throughout the 1950s, the American military developed more
sophisticated nuclear and traditional weapons, including more
powerful missile systems, to meet the Soviet threat. The Soviets
did the same as they poured their nation's resources into armaments. Each country adopted a policy of massive retaliation should
the other strike first. The balance of power was replaced by a balance of terror.

To help diffuse the intense atmosphere both superpower leaders
began to hold face-to-face meetings. These "summit conferences"
provided the opportunity for each side to assess the other. Although some successes resulted, the meetings were primarily me-
dia events. In July 1955 President Eisenhower and Soviet
Communist party chairman Khrushchev met at a summit conference in Geneva, Switzerland. While the Soviet leader did not accept the American proposal for "open skies" inspection of each
other's country by surveillance aircraft to prevent a surprise attack, he did agree that nuclear war would be a disaster for both
sides.

The race to build technology and assert military dominance
reached a new peak in 1957. That year the Soviet Union stunned
the world with the launching of Sputnik I, the first artificial satellite to orbit the earth. The Soviet achievement sent shock waves
throughout America. Many incorrectly thought it symbolized an
overwhelming Soviet missile superiority. Fear of imminent nuclear
war permeated society and led to frenzied activities on all fronts. A
bomb shelter building craze erupted, with nearly one million family shelters built by 1960. In schools children jumped under desks to
practice "duck and cover" during air-raid drills. Highways leading

out of major cities were declared "Civil Defense Evacuation Routes," to be used as escape routes to less populated areas.

The world lurched from one heart-stopping event to another. A second Berlin crisis was created, when, in 1958, Khrushchev decided to use the illusion of Soviet nuclear superiority to force the United States and its allies to relinquish control over West Berlin.[4] As the crisis deepened, the then junior senator from Massachusetts, John F. Kennedy, spoke on the Senate floor in August 1958 about the dangers:

> *Surely we realize that the possibilities of serious miscalculation of war by inadvertence, of having both sides caught in a course which would lead to an all-out war which neither originally contemplated, of the calling of a bluff or of a sudden spreading of a nuclear war . . . Let no one think . . . that a Soviet attack, inadvertent or otherwise, is impossible.[5]*

The West held fast and refused to bargain with the Soviets over Berlin. The crisis eased and the Soviets lessened the pressure. In 1959 the United States turned its attention to electing a new president. With the inauguration of John F. Kennedy in January 1961 as president of the United States, pressure on Berlin again increased as Khrushchev tested the new leader's resolve. Thousands of East Germans, seeking a better life in the West, fled to West Berlin in a steady stream. Embarrassed at the sight of its citizens fleeing Communist rule, the Soviets ordered the construction of the Berlin Wall to seal the border between East and West Berlin. The wall stood until 1989 as a symbol of cold war hostilities and the division of Germany into democratic and communist states.

As powerful a symbol as the Berlin Wall was of the cold war, its construction was not nearly as explosive as an event closer to U.S. shores. The happenings on the island of Cuba, a then internationally insignificant country just ninety miles from the United States, nearly plunged the world into nuclear war. There, after seizing power in 1959, Fidel Castro established the first openly Communist government in the Western Hemisphere. Events on the island soon brought both superpowers to the brink of nuclear war.

Two

AND IN THIS CORNER

❖ ❖ ❖

"We will bury you."
(NIKITA KHRUSHCHEV)

*"Our goal is not the victory of might, but the
vindication of right."*
(JOHN F. KENNEDY)

No two world leaders were more dissimilar. Nikita Khrushchev, born in 1894 to illiterate Russian peasants, began life as a shepherd's assistant. His formal education ended in elementary school. He couldn't write a speech without grammar and spelling mistakes. John Fitzgerald Kennedy, son of a wealthy Irish-American family, never worked when he was a child. He graduated from Harvard University and was a recipient of the prestigious Pulitzer prize for his book *Profiles in Courage*.

When Nikita was fourteen years old the family moved to the coal-mining area of the Ukraine. Nikita followed his father into the coal pits, where the working conditions were harsh. A friend introduced the boy to the Communist Manifesto (the classic document of Communist theory) and the young mine worker became a leader of strikes and demonstrations. During the Russian Revolution in 1917, Nikita joined the Red Guard and began a successful career as a Communist party functionary.

In 1922 the party sent Khrushchev to Moscow to study at a mining institute. There he served as the school's political leader. His dedication was noticed by party leaders, and Khrushchev was rewarded with increasingly important assignments. He was involved in the building of the Moscow subway system, a showplace to the world for Communist planning and ingenuity. For his efforts Khrushchev was awarded the Order of Lenin, a distinguished honor. Khrushchev proved particularly adept at avoiding the party infighting that cut short the careers (and lives) of other ambitious officials. Even as his colleagues were experiencing Stalin's infamous purges and show trials, Khrushchev continued to rise steadily among the Soviet power elite. In 1939, when over 150,000 party functionaries were arrested by Stalin, Khrushchev was elected to the politburo, the central governing body of the Communist party and, in essence, of the Soviet Union. Thus he became one of the ten most influential Soviet leaders.

By the late 1930s war with Germany seemed unavoidable. Khrushchev was elected acting first secretary of the Ukrainian Communist party. When the Germans invaded the Soviet Union in 1941, he was put in charge of the defense of Kiev, the largest city in the Ukraine. After the war Khrushchev faced major problems with agriculture in the Ukraine, with resulting famine and political unrest. The Ukraine is the "breadbasket" of the region and was important to the economic well-being of the Soviet Union. Khrushchev was removed from his leadership role for a time but managed to return to power in 1949 as first secretary of the Moscow Communist party, a prestigious post.

In the 1950s Khrushchev continued to refine his survival skills in the paranoid world of Stalinist politics. Although victorious in the war against Germany, Stalin grew increasingly suspicious of others. His series of purges and the fear they caused consumed governmental and party leaders. Millions of Soviet citizens were exiled to *gulags*—the harsh, isolated work camps in remotest Siberia. With Stalin's death in 1953 members of the Communist party elite breathed a collective sigh of relief and began jockeying to succeed him. The collective leadership that replaced Stalin's one-man rule gave way to the eventual rise of a single dominant figure. That person was Nikita Khrushchev. Anxious to ease the harshness and fear that had prevailed during the Stalin era, Khrushchev appeared before the 20th All Union Congress of the Communist Party in 1956 to make the most controversial speech of his career.

Choosing as his topic "On the Cult of Personality," Khrushchev denounced the cruel and dictatorial edicts of Stalin as criminal acts. The delegates "listened in shocked silence, only occasionally interrupting the speaker with exclamations of amazement and indignation" as Khrushchev spoke of the illegal mass repressions sanctioned by Stalin.[1] Later, when a delegate asked why those in leadership roles during the Stalin era didn't do anything to halt the excesses of power, Khrushchev honestly replied, "We were frightened to stand up against Stalin."[2]

By 1958 Khrushchev was both premier of the Soviet Union and head of the Communist party. As leader, he was concerned about agricultural problems and set as a goal the improvement of the Soviet standard of living. At the same time, he wanted the world to view the Soviet Union as a true superpower, equal to the United States in accomplishment and prestige. His theme of "peaceful coexistence" with the Western democracies was an attempt to encourage the Soviet people to pursue a better life-style while conveying a peaceful image abroad. In July 1955 Khrushchev met in Geneva, Switzerland, with President Eisenhower at a summit conference that helped to defuse the harsh relations between the two countries.

The successful launching of Sputnik I in 1957 shocked the West but had the opposite affect in the Soviet Union. Although the Soviets still lagged pitifully behind the United States in food and consumer products, the scientific accomplishment of Sputnik boosted Soviet morale and secured Khrushchev's leadership.

Even with the successes in the space program, Khrushchev could not erase the image of the Soviet Union as an international bully. When Hungary's Communist leadership permitted a pro-democracy movement in 1956 to initiate a change in government, the Soviets could not ignore the threat to their own power. Khrushchev, facing harsh criticism from the West, sent Soviet tanks and troops into Budapest to brutally crush the rebellion. Thousands of

Hungarian "freedom fighters" were killed; many others escaped to the West. Television news pictures of the repression only heightened the anti-Communist fervor in the United States.

In 1959 Khrushchev became the first Soviet leader to visit the United States. He had a deep-seated inferiority complex, but met eagerly with President Eisenhower. The press later gushed about the new and friendly "spirit of Camp David."[3] The Soviet leader did not have the calm and dignified presence of Eisenhower. He dressed in baggy plain suits and radiated the image of a simple, earthy peasant as he traveled through America dispensing messages to friendly crowds about "peaceful coexistence." Gone was his highly publicized threat to America of "we will bury you." His major disappointment was not being allowed to visit Disneyland, for security reasons.

Senator John F. Kennedy, in a speech on October 1, 1959, at the University of Rochester, cautioned Americans about Khrushchev, whom he had briefly met at a Washington meeting during the trip:

> . . . *Mr. Khrushchev is no fool—and the American people now know that beyond a doubt. He is shrewd, he is tough, he is vigorous, well informed, and confident . . . There was some feeling in recent years that even Mr. Khrushchev could be pictured largely as a short-tempered, vodka-drinking politician-buffoon.*
>
> *But the Khrushchev with whom I met . . . was a tough-minded, articulate, hard-reasoning spokesman . . .*[4]

The era of improved relations ended abruptly in May 1960 just as Khrushchev and Eisenhower were about to meet at another summit, this time in Paris. Earlier that month the Soviets shot down a high-flying United States photographic reconnaissance plane, called the U-2,[5] while it was spying over Soviet territory. At first, thinking the plane and its pilot had been destroyed in the crash, the United States denied the spying allegations. When the Soviets then produced the plane's pilot, Francis Gary Powers, shaken but alive, President Eisenhower admitted the truth of the plane's mission, but he refused to apologize to the Soviets. Khrushchev left

Paris in a huff without ever meeting with Eisenhower, and the cold war struggles continued.

Khrushchev next returned to the United States in September 1960 to attend the opening session of the United Nations. His image as an unpolished bully resurfaced as he unexpectedly removed his shoe and banged it loudly on the table in front of him during a formal speech by Britain's prime minister. People around the world were amused and concerned with this strange behavior and the breech of etiquette did nothing to endear Khrushchev to the diplomatic world. The Soviet leader's rudeness contrasted sharply with the public image of the new United States president.

John F. Kennedy was born in Brookline, Massachusetts, on May 29, 1917, into a large, competitive family. His father, a shrewd businessman who became a multimillionaire, was named United States ambassador to Great Britain by President Franklin Roosevelt in the 1930s. John graduated from Harvard University in 1940. His honors thesis, *Why England Slept*, an analysis of the British appeasement policy toward the Nazis, was published that same year and became a national best-seller. Kennedy served as a United States Navy officer in the Pacific during World War II and commanded a small PT boat, which was sunk by the Japanese. Escaping with his life, the injured young officer successfully rescued his crew. Years later a high school student asked the presidential candidate, "How did you become a hero?" Kennedy answered simply, "It was absolutely involuntary. They sank my boat!"

First elected to Congress from Massachusetts in 1946, he was reelected in 1948 and 1950. In 1952 he was elected to the United States Senate. His book on American political heroes, *Profiles in Courage*, written while he was recovering from back surgery, was awarded the Pulitzer prize in 1957. Although he suffered most of his life with back pain and the debilitating results of Addison's disease, Kennedy never lost optimism about the future. He was articulate, handsome, and smart. In 1956 he lost the Democratic nomination for vice president but bounced back four years later with one of the most energetic presidential campaigns in history. When John Kennedy defeated Vice President Richard Nixon to be-

During the Crisis, President Kennedy (back to camera) relied on the ad-vice of his cabinet and aides. Shown here with the president are McGeorge Bundy on the left, General Maxwell Taylor, and Secretary of Defense Robert McNamara on the right.

come president of the United States in 1960, no one was happier than Khrushchev. The Soviet leader hoped Kennedy would display less rabid anti-Communism than Nixon, who was long associated with "anti-Red" causes.

The new administration was quickly defined by the youth, vi-brancy, and intellect of the advisers appointed by the new presi-

President Kennedy walking with Theodore Sorensen, a close adviser and the president's speechwriter.

dent. Kennedy surrounded himself with the best minds in the country. As special assistant for national security, he appointed McGeorge Bundy, the thirty-four-year-old dean of Harvard College who was a nationally known professor and writer in the field of government. Arthur Schlesinger, historian and writer, served as a White House aide. Walt Whitman Rostow advised the president on foreign affairs. Kennedy's speechwriter and special assistant was Theodore Sorensen, a long time friend and trusted aide.

When Kennedy came to office, there was much unrest in the world. Civil wars were being fought in many countries that were once colonies of Western democracies. In the Congo, Vietnam, and

Laos, revolutionary armies of national liberation fought against the established, mostly Western-oriented governments. Many revolutionaries were Communist-inspired and were supported by the Soviet Union. Yet some revolutions seemed to begin simply as a way for powerless people to remove the excesses of corrupt and uncaring governments. Such was the case in Cuba, at least at first.

From the moment Fidel Castro seized power in Cuba in 1959, there was a gnawing uneasiness about his politics. Many wealthy and middle-class Cubans fled. After Castro openly aligned his country with the Soviet Union and the Communist world, President Kennedy ended diplomatic relations with Cuba and ordered a halt to the importation of sugar, Cuba's main cash crop. Most Americans could not tolerate an avowed Soviet satellite as a neighbor. In southern Florida an active and vocal Cuban exile community emerged, which dreamed of a quick overthrow of Castro.[6] With the financial support and military training of the United States Central Intelligence Agency, paramilitary exile groups prepared for an invasion of Cuba.

By the time John F. Kennedy took office in January 1961, all plans for the invasion of Cuba by exile troops were complete. The new president was briefed and accepted assurances of success from the Department of Defense and CIA leaders. As the time approached for the invasion to take place, Kennedy began to doubt the advisability of direct United States military involvement. "The minute I land one Marine," he said, "we're in this thing up to our necks. I can't get the United States into a war, and then lose it."[7]

As military and intelligence advisers continued to champion the invasion, Kennedy continued to ponder the United States military commitment. He feared the certain response of the Soviet Union, which, in the fragile atmosphere of the cold war, could widen this limited action. The Soviets could bolster the Cubans with an influx of "volunteer" soldiers or increase tension in Berlin. When the Cuban exiles finally landed at the Bay of Pigs on April 17, 1961, they met with total disaster. Stranded on the beaches without hope of reinforcements and deprived of U.S. Air Force cover flights, the hapless exiles were easily defeated by the Cuban army. When the smoke had cleared, 114 invaders lay dead on the beaches and over 1,100 were taken prisoner. For the president, it was a crushing defeat.

Kennedy and Khrushchev met at a summit conference in Vienna, Austria, in June 1961. Each planned to exert influence on the other, but neither leader truly understood his counterpart. Each used the opportunity to gauge the other's strengths and weaknesses. Khrushchev was at his bullying best. He engaged in homey talk and in his folksy way tried to influence Kennedy. Kennedy responded forcefully with wit. At one photo session Kennedy pointed to two medals Khrushchev was wearing and asked what they were. Khrushchev replied they were Lenin Peace Medals. The president responded, "I hope you keep them."

Kennedy discovered that Khrushchev had a limited understanding of the United States. While Kennedy came prepared to compromise on such crucial issues as nuclear testing and Berlin in order to lessen the threat of war, the Soviets were not prepared to move from their hardened positions. When discussion turned to Berlin, Khrushchev demanded that the United States recognize East Germany as an independent country. Kennedy refused. "We are determined to maintain those rights at any risk," he warned Khrushchev. The summit ended badly, with Khrushchev threatening to sign a separate peace treaty with East Germany by December. Kennedy's response was chilly. "If that is true, it is going to be a cold winter."

When the topic of Cuba came up, Khrushchev said that the Bay of Pigs attack only strengthened the Cuban revolution and Castro. Kennedy responded that the United States had attacked Cuba "because it was a threat to American security." Khrushchev then made an important point. Referring to American missiles based in NATO countries bordering the Soviet Union, the Soviet leader said, "If the U.S. believes it is free to act, then what should the USSR do?. . . The USSR is stronger than Turkey and Iran, just as the U.S. is stronger than Cuba. This situation may cause miscalculation . . ."[8] One of Khrushchev's advisers later said the Soviet leader thought "The Americans had to be put in the same position as the Soviet Union."[9] Berlin was the first test of strength, nuclear weapons and Cuba would soon follow.

In June, 1961, President Kennedy and Chairman Khrushchev met in Vienna, Austria. For the new president, the meeting was not a success. (Left to right: Soviet Foreign Minister Andrei Gromyko, Kennedy, and Khrushchev, wearing his medals.)

Kennedy was inwardly shaken by his meeting with the Soviet leader and determined that the United States had to counteract with toughness. Khrushchev dismissed the American leader as young and inexperienced, unwilling or incapable of standing up to Soviet threats. Within months, Khrushchev began to apply more pressure. Kennedy, in a television broadcast to the nation in July 1961, urged Americans to build bomb shelters.

Khrushchev's public statements about Berlin became even more harsh and threatening. In August 1961, under pressure from the East Germans to stem the flow of its citizens to the freedom of West

Berlin, Khrushchev ordered the erection of the Berlin Wall, dividing the city in two. Between 1945 and 1961 over three and a half million East Germans had escaped to the West through Berlin.

Fearful that American rights in West Berlin were in jeopardy again, as they were in 1948, Kennedy ordered armored trucks and troops to travel by highway through East German territory to West Berlin. In a tense altercation that could have escalated into a wider conflict, American and Soviet tanks faced each other at Checkpoint Charlie, a crossing point from the American sector into East Berlin. With neither side willing to risk a wider war, possibly involving nuclear weapons, each warily backed off and the danger was temporarily defused.

In September the Soviets resumed the testing of nuclear weapons in the atmosphere, something they had promised not to do unless the United States acted first. Khrushchev justified his action by saying, "The Soviet government has been compelled to take this step under the pressure of the policy of leading NATO powers. This aggressive bloc leaves the Soviet Union no other choice."[10] Between September and November the Soviets tested over thirty powerful nuclear weapons. Then, trying to instill an element of fear, Khrushchev added, "No superdeep shelter can save them from an all-shattering blow from this weapon."

Meanwhile, the American public, unaccustomed to international setbacks, focused on the Communist threat closest to their homes—Cuba. Occasional forays by small guerrilla groups into Cuba had an insignificant impact. The burning of a small factory or the detonation of a bomb did little to endanger the Castro regime but lifted the spirits of the Cuban exiles in Miami. While the Kennedy administration instituted top-secret planning to topple Castro, diplomats took the American case against Castro to the Organization of American States (OAS). At a meeting in Uruguay in January 1962 the hemispheric organization of twenty-one countries voted to exclude Cuba "from participation in the inter-American system." Early the next month the president invoked an embargo, officially halting trade with Cuba. Before signing the official proclamation, Kennedy

October, 1961. Soviet and United States tanks face each other in a tension-filled confrontation at Checkpoint Charlie, the American border crossing in Berlin.

sent his press secretary out to buy all the Cuban cigars he could. Thirty years later that embargo was still in force.

Meanwhile, the CIA continued planning the multifaceted Operation Mongoose to topple Castro from power. They established a training center in southern Florida for recruited exiles. The guidelines for the operation indicated that the mission's success would eventually "require decisive U.S. military intervention."[11] Information about Operation Mongoose remained a secret in the United States: the Soviets knew all about it. Cuban intelligence had succeeded in placing their own agents among the exiles training for invasion and sabotage of their homeland. Years later Secretary of Defense MacNamara said, "If I had been a Cuban leader at that time, I might well have concluded that there was a great risk of U.S. invasion."[12]

At the same time, the United States was conducting highly visible military training exercises around the Caribbean. These exercises were intended to send a strong message to Castro and the Soviets about United States power and resolve.

Meanwhile, Nikita Khrushchev was beset by mounting problems in his own country. The agricultural programs he himself had established were not working, and strikes and demonstrations had broken out in scattered cities. With the exception of advances in space research, industrial growth was also lagging. On the international scene the militant Chinese Communists were criticizing Khrushchev's lack of response to the West in Berlin and Cuba. During a vacation on the Black Sea in April, Khrushchev suddenly realized a way to solve his international problems. His plan would make the world think the Soviet Union was the nuclear equal of the United States while providing time to produce enough missiles to balance the U.S. arsenal. Thinking of American nuclear missiles pointing at him from NATO member Turkey, across the Black Sea, Khrushchev decided to station similar missiles in Cuba. Nuclear missiles in Cuba would not only keep the United States from attacking the Communist island but would teach the Americans what it was like to be surrounded by close-range enemy nuclear weapons.

"Why shouldn't the Soviet Union have the right to do the same as America," Khrushchev said to his aides. It was an appealing plan and the Soviet leader moved quickly to implement it. Khrushchev decided it was essential to keep the project completely secret. When Cuba was fully armed it would be too late for the United States to react. There were dissenters in the Soviet government. Foreign Minister Andrei Gromyko told Khrushchev, "Putting our nuclear missiles in Cuba would cause a political explosion in the United States."[13] Khrushchev did not listen. Certain of success, he refused to consider alternate plans of action if the U.S. discovered the missiles before they were fully operational.

The Soviets and Cubans quickly reached agreement on deployment of the nuclear weapons. While shipments of warheads, missiles, and bombers departed Soviet ports, Khrushchev began a long tour of the Soviet Union to keep Western attention away from what was really happening. The Cuban leader, once alerted to the Soviet plan, became even more vocal in his threats toward the United States. In a speech on July 26, 1962, Fidel Castro boasted that "mercenaries" no longer posed a threat to Cuba. Even plans by Kennedy to invade Cuba could not succeed, Castro added, since Cuba had acquired new weapons to beat back any direct attack.

United States intelligence agencies began monitoring the arrival of increasing numbers of Soviet technicians, equipment, and weapons in Cuba. Lulled by the belief that the Soviets wouldn't dare insert offensive nuclear weapons into the Western Hemisphere, alarm bells didn't sound in Washington and the shipments continued.

THREE

THE BUILDUP

❖ ❖ ❖

"Things just aren't right."
(CONGRESSMAN CHARLES HALLECK)

Republican Senator Homer Capehart of Indiana was angry. "How long will the president examine the situation?" he thundered, "Until the hundreds of Russian troops will grow into hundreds of thousands? Whatever happened to the Monroe Doctrine?" The senator was not the only American upset with the news of foreign troops in Cuba. Since 1823 it had been a cardinal principle of American foreign policy not to tolerate the involvement of any European power in the Western Hemisphere. Yet in 1962 Americans followed with incredulity the daily press accounts of a growing buildup of Soviet forces on Cuba, just ninety miles away.

The year 1962 was a congressional election year and the Republicans seized on Cuba as a main campaign issue. Public opinion polls showed a growing concern over Communist domination of Cuba and a dramatic decrease in the president's popularity. As the November elections grew closer, American voters wondered just what was happening in Cuba. At the same time, the jittery public carefully followed the continuing cold war conflicts between the United States and the Soviet Union, especially those involving Berlin and the nagging problems of nuclear weapon testing and proliferation.[1] In spite of the existing global problems, Cuba held everyone's attention.

In the mid 1950s a guerrilla movement, organized by Fidel Castro, was formed to remove the entrenched despotic leader of Cuba, Fulgencio Batista. Batista, in power off and on since 1940, had enriched himself and his followers while ordinary citizens lived in poverty. Until the very end of his rule, when it became clear that Castro's rebels were destined to win, Batista was supported by the United States. Many large American corporations owned important businesses on the island and the United States government had a long-term lease on Guantanamo Bay, which it had turned into a key American military facility.

Most Americans were unsure of Castro's politics even as he assumed power in early 1959. To some he was a charismatic revolutionary who had led a popular uprising against a corrupt dictator. Others, suspicious of his land reform laws, which appropriated the farm holdings of large Cuban and American landowners and seized American-owned oil refineries, saw elements of Communism. Indeed, the Soviet Union openly welcomed the change of governments and began supplying Castro with military and economic aid. By December 1960 Cuba had officially joined the Communist world to become the first Communist country in the Western Hemisphere. The United States quickly ended diplomatic relations with the Castro government.

In July 1960 the United States put an embargo on all trade with Cuba and drastically cut United States imports of Cuba's most important crop, sugar. The Soviet Union responded by promising to buy the sugar from its ally. In addition, the Soviets increased dramatically the amount of foreign aid and equipment. That fall, as the first major Soviet arms shipments began to arrive in Cuba, Khrushchev made it a point to visit Fidel Castro when the two leaders were in New York City to attend that year's opening session of the United Nations.

The vocal Cuban exile community in the United States continued to fuel the flames of anti-Castroism in the United States.

Their goal was nothing less than the immediate overthrow of Castro and a return to their homeland. With the help of the United States, exile guerrilla bands engaged in hit-and-run attacks on Cuba.

For President Kennedy the Bay of Pigs disaster in April 1961 raised the risk of an accidental war with the Soviet Union. As hundreds of out-maneuvered Cuban exiles were pinned down on the beach by Castro's troops, Khrushchev sent an ominous warning to Kennedy threatening to give Castro "all necessary assistance." In return, Kennedy had no choice but to warn the Soviet leader that the United States would not tolerate outside military intervention in Cuba.[2] Yet he was careful not to escalate the incident into a major confrontation between the two superpowers.

Even when it was obvious that the exiles were doomed without air cover, Kennedy refused to allow American planes to strike at Cuba. On the beach the CIA-trained exiles were dumbfounded. "You can imagine how we felt," one brigade member later said, "We thought it was treason."[3] The survivors spent nearly two years in Cuban jails until Castro freed them in return for millions of dollars in American medical and food aid.

President Kennedy was also stunned by the disaster. "How could I have been so stupid," he told Theodore Sorensen. The new president learned an important lesson. He could not rely on the exclusive advice of the professional military and intelligence "experts" at the Pentagon and the Central Intelligence Agency. For the remainder of his administration he would turn instead to the close group of carefully selected advisers whose judgment he respected. Speaking on television to the American public, the president promised, "We intend to profit from this lesson . . . We intend to intensify our efforts for a struggle in many ways more difficult than war."[4]

Concern about Cuba intensified as secret plans to overthrow Castro were developed in Washington. In a report to Kennedy presidential adviser Walter Rostow listed five threats to America by the Castro regime:

a. It might join with the USSR in setting up an offensive air or missile base.
b. It might . . . threaten . . . other Latin American nations.
c. It might develop its covert [secret] subversive network in ways which would threaten other Latin American nations from within.
d. Its ideological contours are a moral and political offense to us.
e. Its . . . success may tend to inflame disruptive forces in the rest of Latin America . . .[5]

Reacting to the perceived threats, the United States instituted a number of diplomatic and political operations, Operation Mongoose contained a variety of plans to "help the people of Cuba overthrow the Communist regime from within Cuba and institute a new government with which the United States could live in peace."[6] Unfortunately for President Kennedy, the plan was long on theory but short on delivery.

At the summit conference in Vienna, Austria, in June, Khrushchev battered the American president with threats and bombast. Seizing the opportunity, Nikita Khrushchev quickly began sending Soviet "technicians" and weapons to Cuba. By August 1962 reports from Cuban refugees and CIA agents indicated a growing buildup of Soviet troops and sophisticated weaponry on the island. In addition, intelligence sources learned that civilians were being evacuated from certain areas where property was being seized and cleared for construction. A high-level United States photographic reconnaissance flight over the eastern part of Cuba produced startling news. "I've got a SAM site," a sharp-eyed analyst shouted as he examined freshly arrived photographs. For the first time, concrete evidence existed of defensive Soviet surface-to-air missiles (SAMs) on Cuban soil.

Keeping the news secret was not easy. The Republicans realized the political advantage of criticizing the Democratic president's Cuban policy. On August 31 Senator Kenneth Keating of New York rose to speak on the floor of the United States Senate.

I am reliably informed that between August 3 and August 15 at the Cuban port of Mariel, ten to twelve large Soviet vessels anchored at the former Maranta docks. The Soviet ships unloaded 1,200 troops. . . What are the Soviets planning to do with their new island fortress?[7]

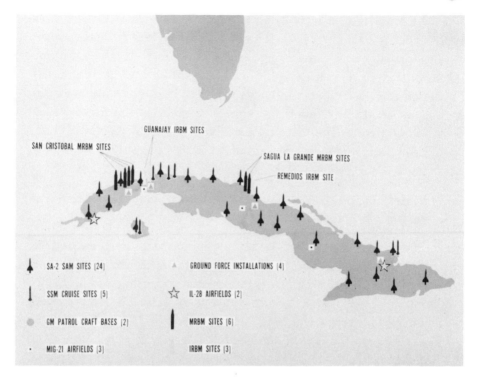

A map of Cuba showing the Soviet military buildup on the island during the crisis. Cuba bristled with Soviet weapons. Notice the proximity of Cuba to Florida, at the top of the map, only 90 miles away.

Cries intensified in the United States for action against Cuba. Kennedy tried to squelch the emotional war talk. He was aware of the international implications of military action against Cuba and the Soviets. Yet he did not want to appear weak, so he issued statements to the press promising to act on Cuba, if and when it became necessary. *The New York Times*, analyzing the situation, concluded that the president had two major options. The first was a naval blockade of Cuba to halt the Soviet buildup of troops and weapons. The second was an invasion to take over the island. Either action could provoke a world war involving nuclear weapons.

At American bases on islands in the Caribbean, United States Marines practiced realistic landings on the beaches to simulate an actual attack on Cuba. People found it amusing that the code name for one exercise was Ortsac, Castro spelled backward. In spite of the military activity on and around Cuba, Kennedy's advisers did not anticipate any immediate danger to the United States. In a memorandum to the national security adviser, McGeorge Bundy, Arthur Schlesinger, special assistant to the president, wrote:

> *Any military construction will probably be defensive in function: a launching pad directed against the United States would be too blatant a provocation.* [8]

Schlesinger concluded that the construction was related to eavesdropping on communications at Cape Canaveral, the launching site for the U.S. space program, or perhaps to plans for shooting down overflying American U-2s. The U-2 flights had recently discovered the growing network of SAM missile sites. Nevertheless, Bundy recommended increased surveillance of Soviet shipments to Cuba and preparation of contingency plans should Soviet nuclear weapons also be found.

Bundy and others recommended that the president "draw the line" by making it absolutely clear to the Soviets that the United States would not tolerate installation of nuclear weapons and long-range missiles in Cuba.

In a secret memorandum on August 22, 1962 [9] the CIA concluded that the recent arrival in Cuba of increasing numbers of personnel and equipment from Soviet bloc nations was unprecedented. "Clearly something new and different is taking place. As yet limited evidence suggests that present activities may include the augmentation of Cuba's air defense system, possibly including the establishment of surface-to-air missile sites . . ." The same memo also reported increased sightings by recent refugees from Cuba of military construction at heavily guarded sites around the island.

Public pressure for action increased on the president. At his September 4, 1962, news conference Kennedy issued a public statement not only to calm nervous Americans but to warn the Soviets:

*There is no evidence of any organized combat force in Cuba from
any Soviet bloc country . . . of the presence of offensive ground to
ground missiles: or of other significant offensive capability . . .
were it to be otherwise, the gravest issues would arise.*[10]

In truth, the president's statement was geared more toward
American voters than the Soviets. Kennedy and his advisers could
not imagine that the Soviets would "do anything as crazy . . . as
placement of Soviet nuclear weapons in Cuba."[11]

The president had made a clear distinction. He would tolerate
defensive weapons in Cuba but not weapons that could inflict damage on the United States. He obviously recognized the danger of
forcing the Soviets to remove defensive weapons from Cuba. Kennedy was not willing to risk a war over weapons that were defensive. History had shown how, during the post World War II years,
the United States, with the help of its NATO allies, had ringed the
Soviet Union with hundreds of offensive nuclear weapons. To deny
the Soviets defensive weapons in Cuba would not be understood by
the rest of the world.

On September 6 Theodore Sorensen, the special counsel to the
president, met with Soviet ambassador Anatoly Dobrynin to talk
about the arms buildup in Cuba. The ambassador told Sorensen
there was nothing to worry about and warmly assured him that the
buildup was strictly defensive. Dobrynin even passed on a special
message from Nikita Khrushchev for the president:

*Nothing will be undertaken before the American Congressional
elections that could complicate the international situation or ag-
gravate the tension in the relations between our two countries . . .
provided there are no actions taken on the other side which would
change the situation.*[12]

Yet, to deflect criticism that he was not taking Cuba seriously,
President Kennedy, on September 7, requested and received nearly
unanimous congressional consent to call up fifteen thousand army
reservists in the event they were necessary. The Soviet Union an-
grily labelled the action a "provocation against peace" and issued
an appeal to the United States "to display common sense, not to

lose self control." The arming of Cuba, the Soviets repeated, was "designed exclusively for defensive purposes. How can these means threaten the United States?" The same day Ambassador Dobrynin repeated to United States ambassador to the United Nations, Adlai Stevenson, that "only defensive weapons are being supplied [to Cuba]."

Behind the scenes, Robert Kennedy, attorney general of the United States and brother of the president, called upon Dobrynin. He told the ambassador how angry the president was about the continuing arrival of military aid to Cuba. Dobrynin passed on a letter of reassurance from Khrushchev that no ground-to-ground[13] offensive weapons were being sent to Cuba. On September 11 TASS, the Soviet news agency, reported, "The government of the Soviet Union . . . states there is no need for the Soviet Union to site weapons in any other country (Cuba for instance)."[14]

In spite of the continuing Republican rumblings and shrill calls for immediate military action, the president stood fast. "If at anytime the Communist buildup in Cuba were to endanger or interfere with our security," he said at a September 13 news conference, ". . . this country will do whatever must be done to protect its own security and that of its allies." As a follow-up to a later question, he added, ". . . if Cuba should possess a capacity to carry out offensive actions against the United States, the United States would act."

Unaware of Khrushchev's secret promise as delivered to Robert Kennedy by Ambassador Dobrynin, Republican senators continued to hammer away at Kennedy and the Democrats by providing specific information about the buildup in Cuba. Congressman Charles Halleck, the Republican leader in the House of Representatives, joining the call for action, could only say, "Things just aren't right."

Throughout September and early October, Cuba remained the main issue of the election campaign. On September 26 the House of Representatives, by a vote of 384 to 7, passed a Joint Resolution previously adopted by the Senate. This resolution gave permission for the use of force to defend the Western Hemisphere from Cuban military attack or subversion. In early October the United States

On the portico of the White House President John F. Kennedy and Attorney General Robert Kennedy confer. The president relied heavily on his younger brother to carry out behind-the-scenes diplomacy with the Soviets.

declared that any ships calling upon Cuba would not be allowed to dock at American ports. Attention was diverted only temporarily to other headline-grabbing issues, such as the violence in integrating the University of Mississippi, a revolt in the Congo, and the orbiting of the earth by an American astronaut, Commander Walter Schirra. Then the focus of attention returned to Cuba. As tension grew, the Kennedy administration continued to insist that although Cuba was being dramatically armed by the Soviet Union it was strictly for defense. Without any conclusive proof of offensive capability, the United States had no legal or moral grounds for a military reaction.

FOUR

PICTURES DON'T LIE

❖ ❖ ❖

"We know everything."
(DEAN RUSK)

"I don't know anything."
(ANDREI GROMYKO)

C olonel Oleg Penkovsky was the perfect spy. He was a high-ranking officer in the Soviet intelligence service, with access to valuable secret information about advanced weapons, especially missiles. Beginning in 1961, the colonel supplied the United States and Great Britain with thousands of frames of microfilmed Soviet military secrets, including data on that country's latest intercontinental missiles. The information he and others supplied were pieced together, cataloged, and analyzed by American intelligence officers.

In a rundown section of Washington, D.C., occupying the fourth through the seventh floors of the Steuart Building at the corner of 5th and K Streets, NW, were the offices of the National Photographic Interpretation Center (NPIC). Staffed by experts from the major military and civilian intelligence services of the United States, its mission was to analyze reconnaissance photographs taken from high altitudes. The director of the center was Arthur C. Lundahl, who oversaw a talented force of specialists in photographic interpretation.

Today a network of reconnaissance satellites crisscrosses the earth. The optics they employ are so sophisticated that no place on the planet is immune. The prying eyes of computer-enhanced cameras provide intelligence communities with information previously unavailable. Back in the early 1960s, before these "spy" satellites, high-flying aircraft, outfitted with specially designed cameras and lenses, routinely overflew areas of American concern. Unlike today's satellites, their flight patterns were limited by political decisions and adverse flying conditions. One such high-flying U-2 spy plane, shot down over the Soviet Union in 1960, scuttled a summit conference between Khrushchev and Eisenhower. As a result, agreement was reached to halt such intelligence-gathering flights over Soviet territory. But American intelligence had already learned much from previous flights about Soviet troop and missile deployments. U-2 flights, however, continued over other countries.

As the buildup of Soviet military shipments continued through the summer of 1962, Cuba became a prime target of U-2 overflights. By mid-August agents on the ground in Cuba reported the arrival and the transporting and assembling of Soviet missiles on the island. Since construction of missile launch sites followed a preordained configuration on the ground, the results of high-altitude photography of Cuban sites were matched with previously taken pictures of existing sites in the Soviet Union. The comparisons revealed similar construction patterns. For the first time, there was a strong possibility of Soviet SA-2, surface-to-air missile (SAM) launch sites in Cuba.[1]

At the same time, the increased traffic of Soviet shipping bound for Cuba was closely observed by reconnaissance aircraft. To a casual observer the sight of large shipping crates lashed to the deck of a Soviet freighter would not be very informative. To the trained photo analysts, experts in the newly created art of "cratology," each box told a specific and disturbing story. By matching the individual box types visible on freighter decks to boxes previously photographed as they were being unloaded at other ports, the analysts were able to identify the contents. Missile equipment and bomber airplane parts were among the cargoes thus identified.

Toward the end of August the Central Intelligence Agency issued a secret report of the activity in Cuba. It noted that an "unusually large number of Soviet ships have delivered military cargoes to Cuba since late July and that some form of military construction is underway at several locations in Cuba by Soviet bloc personnel." The report estimated the number of newly arrived Soviet personnel on the island at five thousand.[2] Later, that estimate was increased to ten thousand.[3] The report continued: "There is strong evidence that their mission is related to unidentified military construction."

The report also contained information gleaned from recent refugees about new military construction sites in Cuba. Eyewitnesses reported that "much of the transportation was done at night and even that town street lights were turned off as the convoys passed through . . . What the construction activity involves is not yet known." The report concluded: "Clearly something new and different is taking place."[4]

Alone among the leadership in Washington to suspect the worst was John McCone, director of the Central Intelligence Agency. After studying CIA reports on Soviet ships heading to Cuba, he concluded that the Soviets intended to install offensive missiles on that island. Over objections from others in his agency, McCone, with no hard evidence to back up his theory, sent a memo about his belief to the White House. In response President Kennedy instructed his National Security Council to develop a contingency plan based on McCone's theory. When the first SAM missile sites were discovered, McCone's position further hardened. He reasoned that the Soviets would not go to the trouble and expense of installing defensive missiles all over Cuba if there was nothing valuable there to protect.

The president, trying to calm fears, clearly defined the arms buildup in Cuba for Americans:

Information has reached this Government in the last four days from a variety of sources which established without doubt that the Soviets have provided the Cuban government with a number of anti-aircraft defensive missiles with a slant range of twenty-five miles which are similar to early models of our Nike.[5]

The Soviets, in turn, continued to state that no offensive weapons were being sent to Cuba but warned that an attack by the United States on Cuba or upon Soviet ships bound for Cuba could start a nuclear war. As the CIA continued making plans to implement Operation Mongoose, the number of sabotage and hit-and-run attacks by American-equipped exiles on Cuban targets intensified. A bombing at a Cuban copper mine and strafing attacks from speedboats on seaside hotels did not inflict major damage, but kept the Cubans on edge. Invasion fears grew and Cubans and Soviets expected a major attack at any time, not from inexperienced exiles alone, as in the Bay of Pigs disaster, but by highly trained and equipped United States troops.

Khrushchev had cleverly orchestrated his arms buildup in Cuba to disguise the inclusion of offensive missiles and nuclear weapons. In May 1962 he had sent a high-level delegation to Cuba to propose the placement of nuclear weapons on the island. Over the next few months both countries worked out the details of a treaty to deploy the nuclear weapons, under Soviet control. Interestingly, the Cubans initially proposed that the deployment be made public as a way of preventing an American attack. The Soviets disagreed. Khrushchev wanted to confront the Americans with an accomplished fact.

The United States was aware of the July visit to Moscow by Defense Minister Raúl Castro, brother of the Cuban dictator. The initial impression was of an unsuccessful meeting. Once the arms buildup began, that assessment was revised. "It now appears," Arthur Schlesinger wrote to McGeorge Bundy, "that Raúl succeeded and that the USSR may have decided to make a major investment in Cuba."[6]

On September 25, 1962, Castro proudly announced that the Soviets would build a new fishing port for the Cubans just north of the American-occupied Guantanamo Bay base. American intelligence experts were not convinced of the projected port's peaceful mission. It could be a perfect location for a Soviet submarine base. Eyewitness reports from refugees and agents on the ground in Cuba continued to provide additional information about newly arrived

KASIMOV WITH IL-28 FUSELAGE CRATES ENROUTE TO CUBA
28 SEPTEMBER 1962

The Soviet ship Kasimov *with IL-28 bomber fuselage crates, September 28, 1962. American reconnaissance flights tracked Soviet shipping to Cuba. Intelligence analysts were able to identify the contents of the shipping crates.*

missiles.[7] On September 28 the "cratologists" identified the contents of boxes lashed to the deck of the Soviet ship *Kasimov*. Based on the knowledge previously assembled about Soviet shipping crates, they identified the contents as IL-28 Beagle bombers,[8] capable of carrying nuclear weapons from Cuba to targets in the United States.

By the end of September 1962, U-2 photographs revealed the first verifiable hint that the buildup in Cuba might not be strictly defensive. Hunched over their stereoscopic magnifiers, the photo analysts at NPIC identified distinctive trapezoidal patterns dug into the earth in western Cuba. Similar markings had been previously seen in the Soviet Union at identified intermediate-missile launch sites. Yet no offensive missiles were actually detected in Cuba at that time.

During the month, attacks on the Kennedy administration by Republican senators Capehart and Keating put the Democrats on the defensive. Despite assurances from the White House that the Cuban crisis was being carefully monitored, Congress passed a nearly unanimous resolution extending broad powers to the president to call up reserve troops and help "freedom loving" Cubans. Guerrilla activities of American-sponsored exiles on Cuban targets continued. The Soviets, meanwhile, continued their denial of offensive missiles in Cuba.

On October 9 Senator Keating, not disclosing his source of information, announced there were at least six intermediate-range intercontinental missile sites being built in Cuba. A day earlier, aware of all the rumors about the continuing military buildup, President Kennedy authorized new U-2 flights over western Cuba, where at least one such offensive missile site was said to be under construction. Bad weather over Cuba prevented the flight from taking off for six days.

Major Richard S. Heyser and Major Rudolph Anderson were the first Air Force pilots to fly U-2 missions. Previously, U-2 flights had been under the direct control of the CIA, which employed its own pilots for the secret missions. During the early morning hours of October 14, Major Heyser piloted U-2 mission 3101 unchallenged over sites in western Cuba. His plane, now on an official Air Force mission, was not armed with bombs but with an array of high-resolution cameras. From his vantage point fourteen miles up, Heyser personally could not see much. The sophisticated cameras he operated, however, could detect newspaper headlines on the ground and recorded everything in their path with magnificent resolution.

Within a few moments of touching down at McCoy Air Force Base in Orlando, Florida, the film cans were removed from Heyser's U-2 and transferred to a waiting military jet for the flight to Washington. Once on the ground in Washington, the film was rushed to the Naval Photographic Intelligence Center in nearby Suitland, Maryland. There, under stringent security, the film was processed and a duplicate set made. The next day, October 15, the processed film

An intelligence photo of a Soviet MRBM taken during a parade in Moscow. Below are the missile's measurements. Such photographs were useful in analyzing the results of U-2 photography over Cuba.

was driven downtown under armed escort to the Steuart Building for analysis.

The staff of the National Photographic Interpretation Center was ready. Three teams of highly trained specialists began analyzing the film frame by frame. Using magnifying equipment, special light tables, and stereo viewers, they painstakingly reviewed every inch of every photograph. They looked for any sign of military activity or construction. One team carefully reviewed the film shot over San Cristobal. To a layperson the telltale sign on the photograph appeared as a four-slash pattern dug into the ground. To the analysts it meant something more significant—obvious preliminary work on a SAM missile site. Lately, discovery of such SAM sites in Cuba was not unusual. However, six large canvas covered objects nearby sparked their curiosity. The analysts figured out the dimensions of the objects but could not identify what they were. One analyst thought they looked like boats, but that idea was quickly ruled out. San Cristobal was too far inland from navigable waters. From their size they could possibly be missiles, but not SAMs. Surface-to-air missiles were much smaller.

Once the analysts had done their work, the film was handed over to a special missile-identification team composed of representatives of the CIA, air force, army, and navy. The team members carefully scanned the photographs of the site and the canvas-covered objects. They agreed that the objects were too large to be SAMs. Another expert was called in who brought with him large "black books" crammed with information about various Soviet missiles. Included was information provided by spy Oleg Penkovsky and photographs of Soviet missiles previously displayed at military parades in Moscow. The expert turned to a picture of a Soviet SS-4 medium-range missile.[9] "This sure looks like it," he said. Arthur Lundahl, Director of the National Photographic Interpretation Center, was called to the room and informed of the startling news. He said, "If there was ever a time I want to be right in my life, this is it."[10] By the time the experts analyzed the remaining film from mission 3101, two more medium-range ballistic missile (MRBM) sites were revealed.

Shortly after 5:30 P.M. on Monday, October 15, Lundahl picked up the phone. The Cuban Missile Crisis had begun.

FIVE

DANGEROUS DECEPTION

❖ ❖ ❖

"I don't think we've got much time on these missiles."
(JOHN F. KENNEDY)

U ntil the telephones began to ring that Monday, October 15, it was a typical early fall evening in Washington. Dean Rusk, the secretary of state, took his call in the butler's pantry next to the State Department's formal dining room. He was hosting an official dinner for West Germany's foreign minister. A few blocks away, the assistant secretary of state for Inter-American Affairs, Edwin Martin, was at the National Press Club addressing members of Sigma Delta Chi, the journalism society. As he told the assembled guests there was no threat from Cuba—"The military build up is basically defensive in nature"—the phone rang. The aide who took the call asked in a low voice, "Is it urgent enough to interrupt?" The caller pointedly admonished him, "For God's sake, no!" The message was certainly important, but public attention was the last thing needed right now.

Roswell Gilpatric, the deputy secretary of defense, was still at home when his phone rang. He was dressing for a dinner party at the official Fort McNair, Washington, residence of General Maxwell Taylor, chairman of the Joint Chiefs of Staff. By the time he reached the fort, he was not in a party mood. As the evening progressed, other guests were discretely summoned away from the party to take their calls. Each returned to the dinner table trying to conceal a worried face. No one spoke of the nature of the calls. Wives and guests lucky enough not to receive calls were puzzled as the early happy tone of the evening grew gradually more somber. John McCone, head of the CIA, was in Seattle, Washington, where he received a cryptic message from his assistant: "That which you always expected has occurred."[1] He took little joy in being proven correct.

McGeorge Bundy, special assistant to the president, was at home hosting a dinner party for the new United States ambassador to France. As the sound of clinking glasses and laughter drifted in from the adjoining room, Bundy took a call from the CIA's Ray Cline. Speaking cautiously, in the event someone might be listening in, Cline told Bundy, "Those things we've been worrying about in Cuba are there." Bundy somberly listened to the words of the caller and asked, "You're sure?" When Cline responded positively, Bundy sighed and hung up the telephone.

It was Bundy's job to inform the president—but not tonight, he decisively decided. To leave his guests suddenly without offering an explanation would only create gossip and unwanted speculation. Furthermore, the president had just returned from a vigorous political campaign trip to New York and was thoroughly exhausted. The news could wait for Tuesday morning. That night, as other high government officials tossed and turned in their beds or remained awake at their desks, the president slept. For the next few weeks John Fitzgerald Kennedy would need all the strength he could muster.

Each of the called officials that Monday night received the same unsettling message. Soviet missiles capable of attacking the United States had been discovered in Cuba. The evidence was clear as a picture.

McGeorge Bundy got an early start on Tuesday morning, October 16. At 8:00 A.M. he was already in his White House basement office, meeting with intelligence officers. After seeing the photographic evidence, he took the elevator upstairs to the first family's private living quarters and entered the president's bedroom. John Kennedy, still in pajamas, was finishing his breakfast and browsing through the morning newspapers. Without much small talk, Bundy came right to the point: "Mr. President, there is now hard photographic evidence that the Russians have offensive missiles in Cuba."[2]

Kennedy did not react. It was now painfully clear that, for months, the Soviet leader had been purposely deceiving the American president. As Bundy took notes, the president took charge and began by scheduling two meetings for later that morning. At 11:00 he met with the CIA deputy director, Marshall Carter, to look at the incriminating photographs for himself. As the president studied the photos spread out in front of him, Carter pointed out the missile launchers and transporters. Kennedy remarked that they "looked like footballs on a football field." Once operational the missiles on that site would be capable of reaching targets eleven hundred miles away. That placed important American population centers, such as Washington, Philadelphia, and New York, at grave risk. Although there was no sign of nuclear weapons, Carter offered the unwelcome assessment that they "soon would be."

The president then directed Bundy to invite to the second meeting, at 11:45, a handpicked group of government officials whose judgment Kennedy trusted. Most already knew about the crisis. They were individually summoned to the White House under the greatest secrecy. As an assembled group they would later be referred to as the Executive Committee of the National Security Council or ExComm, for short.

There were fourteen regular ExComm members and several others who came and went as needed. It was not an officially structured committee with legal standing. Every member, without regard to official rank, was considered an equal participant. Some represented major departments of government responsible for the nation's security. Others were there because of their experience in solving crises. Kennedy had learned a hard lesson during the Bay of Pigs fiasco. In this crisis he would surround himself with

The ExComm at work, October 23, 1962. Throughout the crisis, the president relied on this group of trusted advisers. To the left of President Kennedy is Secretary Rusk, to his right, Secretary McNamara. Robert Kennedy is shown opposite, in the far left of the photo.

advisers he trusted and respected and not blindly accept the advice of the military and diplomatic bureaucracies.

As the Cuban Missile Crisis developed, the following individuals played important roles as full or "visiting" members of the Ex-Comm:

From the State Department:
Dean Rusk, secretary of state
George Ball, undersecretary of state
Edwin Martin, assistant secretary for Latin American affairs
U. Alexis Johnson, deputy undersecretary of state
Llewellyn Thompson, State Department Soviet affairs expert

From the Defense Department:
Robert McNamara, secretary of defense
Roswell Gilpatric, deputy secretary of defense
Paul Nitze, assistant secretary of defense
General Maxwell Taylor, chairman, Joint Chiefs of Staff

From the Central Intelligence Agency:
John McCone, director

Others included:
Robert F. Kennedy, attorney general of the United States
Douglas Dillon, secretary of the Treasury
McGeorge Bundy, the president's national security adviser
Theodore Sorensen, counsel to the president

Visiting members included:
Lyndon B. Johnson, vice president of the United States
Adlai Stevenson, ambassador to the United Nations
Kenneth O'Donnell, special assistant to the president
Dean Acheson, former secretary of state

The first thing President Kennedy ordered was an increase in the number of U-2 flights over Cuba. As a result of these flights, other missile sites were soon discovered, raising the total found to six, including those for longer range intermediate-range ballistic missiles (IRBM). Kennedy then charged the group to put regular work aside and concentrate solely on this problem until they arrived at a solution. All understood that while the president was relying on them to analyze all the possibilities and make recommendations, the ultimate decision of what action to take belonged exclusively to the president.

The group assumed that these newly discovered weapons in Cuba were only the beginning of a larger buildup. The SAM missiles, clearly defensive, were only the first step. Once they were in place to defend the sites, the offensive MRBMs and IRBMs, together with their nuclear warheads, could be safely deployed throughout Cuba without fear of U.S. response. The group concluded that the missiles did not really affect the balance of power:

During the crisis, President Kennedy (left) chats informally with Secretary of Defense Robert McNamara (center) and Chairman of the Joint Chiefs of Staff, General Maxwell Taylor (right).

> *Nevertheless it is generally agreed that the United States cannot tolerate the known presence of offensive nuclear weapons in a country 90 miles from our shore, if our courage and our commitments are ever to be believed by either allies or adversaries.*[3]

The need for utmost secrecy was evident. The president urged all ExComm members to be extremely guarded. If the Soviets knew that the Americans knew, the missiles could be hidden, or at worst, even launched if the missile sites were ready. If the American public found out before the government developed a response, panic could ensue. Not even the wives of ExComm members must be told.

Additional meetings were set for later that day, Tuesday, October 16. For the next six days the committee was in almost constant session either at the State Department or the White House. To

During the week of secret deliberations about the crisis, President Kennedy tried to maintain a normal public schedule. Here he welcomes Astronaut Wally Schirra and his family to the White House just after hearing of the offensive missiles in Cuba.

allow free discussion without the added pressure of his presence, the president decided to attend only selected meetings.

In order not to attract attention, public schedules were carefully maintained. Earlier that morning, after just seeing the photographic evidence, a seemingly relaxed John Kennedy welcomed Mercury astronaut Wally Schirra and his family to the White House for a pleasant meeting. He even took the family outside on a casual stroll to see his daughter Caroline's favorite pony, Macaroni. Later Kennedy met with a panel on mental retardation, signed official proclamations, and hosted an official luncheon for the Crown Prince of Libya. But between scheduled appointments the president kept in telephone contact with his brother, the attorney general. After the Libyan lunch, the president took aside Adlai Stevenson, the United Nations ambassador, and briefed him on the problem: "We'll have to do something quickly . . . the alternatives are to go in by air and wipe them out." Stevenson urged caution: "Let's explore peaceful solutions first." Then the ambassador advised Kennedy not to cancel any public appearances. "That would give alarm," Stevenson said. The president agreed.[4]

The ExComm began to wrestle with the problem at once. The members thought about every option open to the United States, no matter how farfetched. The idea was to leave no possibility unexplored and allow everyone to reach a well-thought-out conclusion. According to Elie Abel,[5] the list of major possibilities included six options:

1. *No action.* Although no one seemed in favor of this option, it would avoid a potential nuclear confrontation. Meanwhile, diplomatic means might be found to defuse the situation.
2. *Diplomatic.* Use the full force of international opinion, including the United Nations, to force the Soviets to remove the missiles from Cuba.
3. *Castro.* Turn directly to Cuba's Castro and warn him of the great danger his country is in.
4. *Blockade.* Use United States naval forces to prevent any offensive missiles and military supplies from reaching Cuban shores.
5. *Air Strike.* Target all the known missile sites with air bombings and destroy the threat at the source.
6. *Invasion.* Launch a full-scale amphibious invasion of Cuba by American soldiers and marines to destroy the sites, overthrow Castro, and restore democracy to the island nation.

By the end of the first day of ExComm meetings, only two possibilities remained as serious options—air strike and blockade. Each had its own pluses and minuses, and debating the merits and failings of each occupied the ExComm members. In spite of the agonizing decision to be made, the prolonged debate provided an opportunity for thorough analysis. It allowed people to rethink their own original positions and consider other options. John Kennedy later said, "If we had to act in the first twenty four hours, I don't think we would have chosen as prudently as we finally did."

The initial response of those at that first meeting, including the president, was to retaliate against the sites with massive air strikes before the missiles were operational. When it was determined that limited air strikes might not destroy all the missiles, expanded massive air strikes were suggested. It soon became clear that no air strike could guarantee one hundred percent success. It also became evident that thousands of Cubans and Soviets would die in the massive downpour of American bombs. The world would condemn U.S. aggression against a small country and the Soviet Union might retaliate in some other way, perhaps by moving against Berlin or attacking U.S. forces elsewhere.

As the air strike discussion became more heated, Robert Kennedy passed a note to Ted Sorensen, "I now know how Tojo felt when he was planning Pearl Harbor."[6] A sneak attack, such as the one Japan engineered against the United States at the beginning of World War II, was not the way Americans acted. As talk veered to and fro among the various military and political options, the president made it clear that he was concerned with only one ultimate outcome, "We're certainly going to do Number One—we're going to take out these missiles."

But time was a major problem. The president himself remarked at the Tuesday morning meeting, "I don't think we've got much time on these missiles . . . maybe we just have to take them out and continue our other preparations . . . we ought to be making those preparations."[7] So while the ExComm continued to meet and debate, United States military forces were quietly assembling in Florida and the Caribbean. Air force bases in Florida, including MacDill Air Force Base in Tampa and Patrick Air Force Base near Cape Canaveral, were placed on full alert. By October 20 two complete U.S. Army divisions had been alerted for immediate movement. As quietly as such a massive movement could be kept, the largest U.S. military mobilization since World War II was taking place in the United States. Civilian airports in Florida were cleared of unnecessary aircraft to make way for the military bombers and fighters. Air defenses and troop deployments were increased at bases in Puerto Rico and at the U.S. naval base at Guantanamo, Cuba. Luckily, the military buildup did not attract much attention because there was a previously scheduled war game exercise taking place in the region, involving a highly publicized flow of troops, planes, and ships—the perfect cover.

The U-2 and other reconnaissance flights over Cuba produced thousands of photographs during the crisis. Each was carefully analyzed and the results passed immediately to the ExComm and the president by Arthur Lundahl. By October 20 a wide array of Soviet offensive weapons had been located. Most alarming was the discovery of a nuclear warhead storage bunker. Unknown at the time was the status of the warheads. The ExComm chose to believe the worst—that nuclear warheads were there. Indeed, years later the Soviets acknowledged that although there were thirty-six warheads on the island at the time of the crisis, none was actually attached to a missile.

On the evening of October 16, when the ExComm reconvened, CIA deputy director Carter reported on the latest reconnaissance from Cuba. Additional offensive missile sites were located but, as yet, no nuclear warheads were seen. In a reflective moment the president thought out loud, "The Russians, I never—now, maybe our mistake was in not saying some time before this summer that if they do this we're [going to] act."[8] There was no time for hindsight; the danger was in the present. Dean Acheson, former secretary of state in the Truman administration, supported the air strike option. According to McGeorge Bundy, Acheson reasoned that "the president had already given fair warning. A military action to destroy these missiles was an entirely legitimate act of self defense and the action should be taken immediately, before the missiles become operational."[9] But the problem with the air strikes remained. They did not guarantee one hundred percent success. Indeed, further study by the Joint Chiefs indicated that any air strike would have to be expanded to include Cuban air force bases and antiaircraft sites.

With the air strike option on everyone's mind, Undersecretary of State George Ball thought through the problem: "What happens beyond that. You go in there with a surprise attack. You put out all the missiles. This isn't the end. This is the beginning."[10] As the discussion continued on the merits of various strategies, Secretary of Defense McNamara raised another alternative for the first time—"a blockade against offensive weapons entering Cuba in the future." By the next day's meetings, the idea of a blockade began to be seriously considered by other ExComm members, including Robert Kennedy and Ted Sorensen. Its basic attraction was flexibility. The United States could begin with a blockade, then add increasing military pressure if no results were produced.

Meanwhile, in Moscow, unaware that his secret plans had been discovered, Khrushchev called in the new American ambassador, Foy Kohler, for a diplomatic discussion. Again the Soviet leader went out of his way to describe the military buildup in Cuba as a defensive matter. In Washington a Soviet official, Georgy Bolshakov, secretly delivered a message to Robert Kennedy on October 17. The message, from Khrushchev, was to be delivered to the president. "Under no circumstances would surface to surface missiles be sent to Cuba."[11]

On Wednesday, October 17, President Kennedy, keeping to a normal public schedule, flew off on a campaign trip to Connecticut on behalf of Democratic state and congressional candidates. The ExComm continued to meet and talk about the choice of air strike or blockade. There were many good reasons for either approach: there were also major problems with each. In an air strike Cuban civilians and Russian advisers would probably die, thereby forcing the Soviets to escalate military action against American targets. Similarly, a naval blockade contained the risk that Soviet ships would have to be sunk automatically, insuring other Soviet actions against American interests. A blockade would also not prevent the Soviets in Cuba from completing the missile sites and firing nuclear weapons at United States targets; it would only prevent new weapons from reaching Cuban shores.

Secretary of Defense McNamara made a strong case for a blockade by arguing that an air strike might eventually be necessary but "let's not start with that course." A blockade would allow the United States to control events by raising the dangers slowly. An initial air strike left no room for compromise.

President Kennedy campaigning, October 19, 1962. During the height of the crisis, Kennedy went on yet another campaign trip. Here he is greeted by a well wisher.

When the president returned to Washington the evening of October 17, Ted Sorensen and Robert Kennedy met him at the airport. As they rode back to the White House, they filled him in on the day's deliberations.

While most Americans were unaware of the crisis, some Washington insiders were beginning to get suspicious. A visiting British general, attending a Pentagon conference, could not help notice that his American hosts kept disappearing for telephone calls and never reappearing at the sessions. Strangest of all, he noticed beds being moved into the offices of top Pentagon leaders. Putting these oddities together, the general concluded that something important was happening.

Perhaps the strangest event of that entire strange week was the

On October 18, 1962, President Kennedy (shown in his favorite rocking chair) met with Soviet Foreign Minister Andrei Gromyko (to the president's right). Seated to the left of Gromyko is Anatoly Dobrynin, the Soviet Ambassador to the United States.

Thursday visit to the White House of Soviet foreign minister Andrei Gromyko. Kennedy and the ExComm group simply didn't know what the Russian wanted. Did he know about the American discovery of missiles in Cuba? Would he bring a new threat from Khrushchev to further inflame the situation? No one knew what to expect. In the event Gromyko knew nothing, Kennedy decided not to tell the diplomat anything about the unfolding crisis. "It was essential," the president said, "that the facts first be disclosed to the American people."

Gromyko was ushered into the Oval Office and took a seat on a sofa next to Kennedy's familiar rocking chair. After some polite discussion about other world events, the conversation shifted to Cuba. Again Gromyko repeated the Soviet claim that the arming of Cuba was strictly defensive. He told Kennedy the Soviet aid was "solely [for] the purpose of contributing to the defense capabilities of Cuba and to the development of its peaceful democracy. If it were otherwise," Gromyko read from his notes, "the Soviet government would have never become involved in rendering such assistance."[12]

Kennedy, with the incriminating U-2 photos in a folder just a few feet away in his desk drawer, sat impassively. He, in turn, read to Gromyko a section from his September 4 statement in which he warned the Soviet Union that the "gravest consequences would follow" if offensive missiles were placed in Cuba. Later Kennedy said, "Gromyko must have wondered why I was reading it but he did not respond."

That evening, as guests arrived at the State Department for a black-tie dinner in honor of Gromyko, the ExComm was about to meet on the floor below. Secretary of Defense McNamara and CIA director McCone entered the ground floor lobby and were instantly besieged by awaiting reporters and photographers there to report on the Gromyko dinner. The two, heading for the ExComm meeting, were not formally dressed, but a reporter casually asked if they were going to the dinner. "Yes," lied McNamara, and the two conspirators headed quickly for the elevator.

While the elegantly dressed guests on the eighth floor ate caviar and toasted each other with champagne, the ExComm members one floor below finally reached majority agreement on a recommended action—a blockade. Those with an opposing view continued to dissent. At nine o'clock the majority group headed to the White House to inform the president. Rather than call attention to themselves by arriving in a convoy of official black cars, they made a quick decision. While Edwin Martin of the CIA walked the few blocks, the others all piled into Robert Kennedy's limousine. The driver, Kennedy, McCone, and Taylor rode in front; six others rode in back, some sitting on the laps of others. One passenger commented, "It will be some story if this car is in an accident."

At the White House the majority group made its case for a naval blockade. The president liked the idea because it provided the Soviets with a way out of the crisis. Work began at once on all the details, including arrangements for a presidential speech to the nation originally set for Sunday night but eventually rescheduled for Monday, October 22. But the president knew the ExComm was not unanimous in its recommendation and that important sentiment still existed for an air strike.

The next morning Kennedy met with the members of the Joint Chiefs of Staff. They urged him to reconsider the air strike or invasion options. The president, already late for another campaign flight, this time to the Midwest, instructed his brother to keep the ExComm deliberating and to call him back to Washington when a final decision was reached.

The ExComm deliberations were taking a toll on the participants. But their mission was not yet complete. Working through the day Friday, they put together two separate scenarios. The first, for a naval blockade of Cuba; the second, for a military attack. Each group then submitted its scenario to the other for criticism and comments. Likewise, Ted Sorensen began writing two versions of the speech the president would deliver on Monday night.

In his notes of the October 20 meeting Ted Sorensen recorded the objections to the air strike option and the advantages of the blockade:[13]

Air Strike
> Inasmuch as the concept of a clean, swift strike has been abandoned as militarily impractical, it is generally agreed that the more widespread air attack will inevitably lead to an invasion with all of its consequences.

Blockade
> It is a more prudent and flexible step which enables us to move to an air strike, invasion or any other step at any time it proves necessary, without the "Pearl Harbor" posture.

The secret deliberations were coming to an end: it was time for a presidential decision.

Six

BLOCKADE

❖ ❖ ❖

"The President may have to develop a cold tomorrow."
(KENNETH O'DONNELL)

Small chinks began to appear in the wall of secrecy surrounding the deliberations of the ExComm. A few reporters began to sense that something important was about to happen. As the circle of government officials who needed to know about the missiles increased, so did the possibility of the news reaching Moscow. On Friday, October 19, Radio Moscow shrilly announced that the highly public American naval maneuvers in the Caribbean were the preparations for an invasion of Cuba.

In Chicago, in the midst of the latest campaign trip on behalf of Democratic candidates, Kennedy realized that time for deliberation was nearly over. Very likely, he would need to return to Washington the next day. Kenneth O'Donnell, the president's aide, turned to the press secretary, Pierre Salinger, who knew nothing of the dramatic events unfolding around him, and made a curious remark: "The president may have to develop a cold tomorrow."

On Saturday morning, with the ExComm decisions firmly in place, the president was called back to Washington. The reporters were dutifully told that Kennedy had a "slight cold" and was going home to recuperate. To continue the charade the usually bare-

Before developing a "slight cold" on a campaign trip to Chicago on October 19, a healthy-looking President Kennedy is shown signing an autograph for two young admirers at a political dinner.

headed Kennedy boarded his airplane wearing a hat. At the same time the president was flying to Washington, American troops around the world were placed on formal alert. The First Armored Division was moving from Texas into Georgia. Naval ships began moving out of their home ports, and air force planes headed out to strategic locations in and around the Caribbean. B-52 bombers, armed with nuclear bombs, were kept in the air in continuous shifts ready to head for preassigned targets in the Soviet Union.

Upon his return to Washington the president went for a swim in the White House pool as Robert Kennedy filled him in on everything that had happened during his absence. Then the president met with the ExComm in the Oval Office. The exhausted members arrived at the White House through different gates to avoid detection by reporters. At that time he again heard the arguments on the two choices for action, a naval blockade or an air strike/invasion. Roswell Gilpatric summed up the choices: "Essentially, Mr. President, this is a choice between limited action and unlimited action: and most of us think that it's better to start with limited action."[1]

After listening to both sides, the president formally decided on the naval blockade. He agreed that beginning with minimal action would allow the United States to increase pressure on the Soviets as needed. He also delayed his scheduled speech to the nation by one day—to Monday—and ordered his staff to make all the detailed arrangements to notify America's allies and to draft all the official documents to support this action. One basic change was made in the terminology. The naval action would be referred to as a "quarantine," since use of the word "blockade" legally meant we would be at war with Cuba.

The next morning, still unsure he had made the right choice, Kennedy invited General Walter Sweeney, commander of the Tactical Air Force, to his office. Again the president asked if an air strike would destroy all the Soviet missiles in Cuba. The general responded that he could not give a one hundred percent guarantee. To the president, General Sweeney's honest assessment confirmed that a quarantine was the only reasonable option.

To throw reporters off the track, important government officials with responsibilities for different areas of the world, began rolling up in their official limousines to the White House west gate, the highly visible entrance used by dignitaries. There was a crisis somewhere, but reporters couldn't figure out where. Meanwhile, unseen by the prying eyes of the press, ExComm members used a little known tunnel from the nearby Treasury Building to gain secret admission to the White House.

At 2:30 P.M., Sunday, October 21, the president convened the first formal meeting of the National Security Council to make official the work of the ExComm.[2] Turning to the chief of naval operations, Admiral Anderson, Kennedy said sympathetically, "It looks as if this is up to the Navy." The admiral simply responded, "Mr. President, the Navy won't let you down."

As the military buildup continued, top secret messages were sent to American ambassadors around the world. Leaders of Congress from both parties were hurriedly called back from their political campaigning and vacations to meet with the president.

Senior American diplomats were hurriedly dispatched around the globe to brief America's allies. Dean Acheson, the former secretary of state who had participated in the ExComm meetings, was sent on the particularly tricky mission of informing France's brittle leader, Charles De Gaulle. In Paris, Acheson explained the American reasons for the quarantine. Offering to show De Gaulle the definitive photographs of the missile sites, the French leader merely brushed them aside, "A great country such as yours does not act without evidence. You may tell your president that France will support him."[3]

The president's speech, "on a matter of highest national urgency," was scheduled for broadcast over all radio and television networks on Monday evening, October 22, at 7:00 P.M. By then everyone knew something was happening, but not what or where. Troop movements attracted a lot of attention. There was speculation all day as to the nature of the crisis. Some correctly assumed it was Cuba, but few realized the seriousness of the situation. Some newspapers were getting too close to the truth, however, and Kennedy himself telephoned the publishers of *The New York Times* and *The Washington Post* and personally requested that they tone down their Monday reporting of the crisis. They agreed.

Meanwhile, the Joint Chiefs of Staff issued an official defense condition alert, raising the worldwide status of all U.S. military forces from the usual peacetime DEFCON 5 to DEFCON 3. It signified the greatest military mobilization in the United States since World War II. U.S. intercontinental-missile-site crews were put on special alert, and missile-launching Polaris submarines set out from their home ports for deployment at sea. The nation's railroads

President Kennedy with Prime Minister Obote of Uganda on October 22, 1962. Just hours before Kennedy's eventful speech, he met with the unsuspecting visitor. Later, after watching the speech on television, Obote remarked how casual the president acted.

were alerted to prepare for the immediate transport of troops and equipment to southern bases.

As additional marine battalions reinforced the United States base at Guantanamo Bay, wives and children were hurriedly evacuated and flown to the U.S. mainland. That same day Colonel Oleg Penkovsky, who had provided the United States with valuable Soviet military secrets, was arrested at his Moscow apartment. He was never seen again. In an interesting and ominous sidelight it was reported years later that just as he was being arrested Penkovsky sent a prearranged secret telephone signal to the United States indicating an imminent Soviet attack. The CIA officials who received the signal did not believe the message and ignored it. Had they believed it, it might have led to U.S. deployment of nuclear bombers over Soviet territory, which could have resulted in a Soviet missile strike in response.[4]

Back in Washington the carefully designed countdown to the president's speech time continued and the circle of informed people grew. As late as 4:00 P.M. on October 22 the president continued to carry on the public duties of his office. He met with the prime minister of Uganda and spent forty-five minutes in deep discussion on the problems of Africa without giving any indication of the impending crisis. In addition, the president signed National Security Action Memorandum 196 formally establishing the legitimacy of the hard-working ExComm. For the duration of the crisis the ExComm was scheduled to meet daily at 10:00 each morning in the Cabinet Room under the direct chairmanship of the president. Cabinet members, congressmen, and diplomats of countries friendly to the United States were all briefed. Not all the congressional leaders supported the idea of a quarantine. Senator Richard B. Russell of Georgia hotly advised the president, "You're going to have to invade Cuba sooner or later. Do it now and you'll have fewer complications."[5]

One hour before Kennedy's scheduled speech, Soviet Ambassador Dobrynin was called into the secretary of state's office and given an advance copy of the speech. Dean Rusk read sections aloud to the shaken ambassador, who then quickly left to inform his government. Rusk informally told the ambassador that it was incomprehensible to him how leaders in Moscow could make such gross errors of judgment as to what the U.S. can accept.[6] Reporters waiting outside described Dobrynin's face as "ashen."

In Moscow the United States ambassador delivered a letter from Kennedy to Khrushchev. In it the president stated a warning and urged caution: "I must tell you that the United States is determined that this threat to the security of this hemisphere be removed ... I hope that your Government will refrain from any

In the most dramatic speech of his career, President Kennedy addresses the nation on Monday evening, October 22, 1962. For the first time he reveals the nature of the danger facing the nation.

action which would widen or deepen this already grave crisis and that we can agree to resume the path of peaceful negotiation."[7]

At the State Department a group of foreign diplomats sat before a television to watch the president's speech. Just before seven o'clock, a commercial message for a bank appeared on the television screen: "How much security does your family have?" The diplomats roared with nervous laughter.[8]

At precisely seven o'clock on the evening of October 22, U.S. jet fighters took off from bases in Florida and headed south on airborne alert. Should Cuba decide to react militarily, they were prepared to respond with force. At the same time, John Fitzgerald Kennedy began his fateful seventeen-minute address:

> *Good evening, my fellow citizens. This Government, as promised, has maintained the closest surveillance of the Soviet military buildup on the island of Cuba. Within the past week, unmistakable evidence has established the fact that a series of offensive missile sites is now in preparation on the imprisoned island. The purpose of these bases can be none other than to provide a nuclear strike capability against the Western Hemisphere.[9]*

Earlier in the week, at an ExComm meeting, the commandant of the Marine Corps had told Kennedy, "You are in a pretty bad fix, Mr. President." To the laughter of others in the room, the president quipped, "You are in it with me."[10] Now the entire country was about to become involved in the most dangerous event the world had ever experienced.

As anxious Americans sat fixed before their televisions and radios, Kennedy bluntly informed the American people about the dangers. "Each of these missiles, in short, is capable of striking Washington, D.C., the Panama Canal, Cape Canaveral . . . Additional sites not yet completed appear to be designed for intermediate range ballistic missiles . . . capable of striking most of the major cities in the Western Hemisphere . . ." He then announced the steps he was taking to remove the threat:

1. A quarantine of Cuba and the turning back of any ship heading to Cuba with "offensive weapons."

MRBM LAUNCH SITE 1
SAN CRISTOBAL, CUBA
23 OCTOBER 1962

MISSILE ERECTOR

CABLE

MISSILE SHELTER TENT

TRACKED PRIME MOVERS

FUEL TANK TRAILERS

The high resolution cameras aboard the U-2 spy plane revealed the construction of Soviet offensive missile sites in Cuba. Photographic analysts studied and labeled the activities they uncovered.

2. An increased surveillance of Cuba.

3. A "full retaliatory attack upon the Soviet Union" by the United States in the event of any launching of Soviet missiles from Cuba at any other country.

4. The reinforcement of the United States Naval Base at Guantanamo Bay.

5. A call for the support of the Organization of American States (OAS).

6. A request for an emergency meeting of the United Nations Security Council.

7. A call upon Khrushchev to "halt and eliminate a reckless and provocative threat . . ."

In his speech that evening President Kennedy drew upon history for a parallel to the situation in Cuba:

> *The 1930's taught us a clear lesson: aggressive conduct, if allowed to go unchecked and unchallenged, ultimately leads to war. This nation is opposed to war. We are also true to our word. Our unswerving objective, therefore, must be to prevent the use of these missiles against this or any other country, and to secure their withdrawal or elimination from the Western Hemisphere.*

"The path we have chosen for the present is full of hazards," Kennedy continued, ". . . and one path we shall never choose, and that is the path of surrender or submission." When the president had finished, Secretary of State Dean Rusk briefly addressed the group of diplomats who had gathered at the State Department to watch the president's address. "We are in as grave a crisis as mankind has been in," he told them.

Even as Kennedy was delivering his speech, Soviet ships were en route to Cuba. "We propose to search them," said a Defense Department spokesman. The secretary general of the United Nations, U Thant, wrote in his memoirs that after watching Kennedy's address he "could scarcely believe my eyes and ears . . . I was more deeply troubled than I had ever been in my life."[11] Around the world people were sobered by the fact that the future of the human race hinged on the actions of two men, Kennedy and Khrushchev. Each had the terrible capability of destroying the world.

In Moscow the initial shock of the discovery of the missiles created a feeling of disbelief. Hours passed with no response from the Soviets. One high-ranking Soviet official said that Khrushchev's first reaction was to order Soviet ships to ignore any blockade and push on through to Cuba. That order was rescinded within a few hours as the seriousness of the situation became clearer. Khrushchev also ordered that construction of the missile sites be speeded up.

Both Kennedy and Khrushchev realized the delicacy of the situation. Neither wanted to box the other into a corner that would not permit a way out of danger. Yet the Soviets found themselves in a difficult situation, especially when photographs of the missile sites were released to the press. Ignoring the photographic evidence on the front pages of newspapers around the world, "Soviet diplomats had to deny, refute and even denounce them, 'proving' to the Americans that there were not missiles at all or not in Cuba at all . . ."[12]

Early the next morning, October 23, Khrushchev responded to Kennedy's speech. The official Soviet position, as transmitted through their TASS news service, was that the U.S. action was nothing more than piracy and a violation of international law that could lead to a nuclear war. A separate letter to Kennedy was, according to the U.S. ambassador, "relatively restrained in tone":[13]

> I must say frankly that the measures indicated in your statement constitute a serious threat to peace and to the security of nations . . . We reaffirm that the armaments which are in Cuba, regardless of the classification to which they may belong, are intended solely for defensive purposes . . .

Khrushchev closed with a warning: "I hope that the United States Government will display wisdom and renounce the actions pursued by you, which may lead to catastrophic consequences for world peace." In Washington the State Department analysis of initial Soviet reaction concluded that "the Soviet Union may be carefully leaving the back door open for a retreat from the danger of general war over Cuba."[14]

At the ExComm meeting the next morning, October 23—the first official one since the crisis began—there was a collective sigh of relief when CIA director McCone reported that no increased alert of Soviet military forces had been detected during the night. Plans were made for increased aerial surveillance over Cuba. When the point was raised that a U-2 might be shot down, the group decided that the U.S. should then retaliate by attacking the Soviet missile site that shot down the plane, but only upon direct orders of the president.

On the diplomatic front meetings were scheduled of both the Organization of American States and the United Nations Security Council. The actual Proclamation of Interdiction, officially announcing the quarantine, was scheduled to be signed that evening,

October 23, by the president. The quarantine would prevent ships from approaching any closer than eight hundred miles to Cuba. In keeping with international law, the quarantine itself would not go into force until 10:00 A.M. (EST) the next day, October 24.

During the 23rd, members of the OAS debated the crisis and then voted unanimously to endorse the U.S. quarantine and condemn the Soviet actions in Cuba. With the support of the Western Hemisphere assured, debate shifted to the United Nations. There U.S. ambassador Adlai Stevenson sharply rebuked the Soviets: "If the United States and other nations of the Western Hemisphere accept this new phase of aggression, we would be delinquent in our obligations to world peace." The Soviet ambassador, Valerian Zorin, responded that the U.S. charges were "completely false."

The ExComm reconvened at 6:00 P.M. The final touches were put on the proclamation the president was about to sign in front of the cameras. In addition, the members approved a response to the letter Kennedy had received from Khrushchev:

> *I am concerned that we both show prudence and do nothing to allow events to make the situation more difficult to control than it already is . . .*

> *I hope that you will issue immediately the necessary instructions to your ships to observe the terms of the quarantine, the basis of which was established by the vote of the Organization of American States this afternoon . . .* [15]

In the Caribbean and southern Atlantic a fleet of United States vessels was in position to effect the quarantine. At 7:06 P.M. President Kennedy entered the Oval Office and to the flash of camera bulbs signed the Proclamation of Interdiction, using his full name, John Fitzgerald Kennedy, something he rarely did.

Even before the crisis the Kennedy administration had opened "back door" communications with the Soviet Union out of public sight. For many reasons, these private channels offered an informal way for both governments to speak easily with each other without the fear of public disclosures. At 9:30 that evening, October 23, Robert Kennedy drove to the Soviet embassy for an "off the

President Kennedy signs the Proclamation of Interdiction on October 23, 1962. The quarantine went into effect the next morning at 10 A.M.

record" talk with Ambassador Dobrynin. Kennedy chastised the ambassador for having told the United States that the Soviets had no intention of placing offensive missiles in Cuba. The placement of those missiles in Cuba, Kennedy told Dobrynin, was "hypocritical, misleading, and false." Dobrynin answered that as far as he knew there were no offensive missiles in Cuba. Dobrynin also said that Soviet captains "have an order to continue their course to Cuba." "Our military vessels have an order of President Kennedy to intercept them," the attorney general responded. "I do not know how this will end," he ominously told the ambassador.

As the attorney general returned to the White House to report to his brother, Dobrynin hurried back to the embassy to send his report to Moscow. International communications were still quite limited in 1962, and Dobrynin later recounted how he had to call the local Western Union telegraph office, which sent a messenger on bicycle: "We gave him the cables. And he, at such a speed—we tried to urge him on—rode back to Western Union, where the cable was sent to Moscow."[16]

As the first Soviet ship drew closer to the interdiction line, eight hundred miles from Cuba, President Kennedy decided to offer the Soviets more time to consider the situation. He called the secretary of defense and shortened the line to five hundred miles. That night lights burned bright in offices all over Washington.

SEVEN

ON THE BRINK

❖ ❖ ❖

*"The cost of freedom is always high—but Americans have always
paid it. And one path we shall never choose, and that is the path
of surrender or submission."*
(JOHN F. KENNEDY)

On Tuesday morning, October 23, U.S. Air Force B-47 bombers and antisubmarine planes landed at Palm Beach International Airport as crowds of curious Floridians gathered along
nearby highways to watch. In southernmost Florida a squadron of
thirteen submarines and a division of destroyers pulled out of the
Key West Naval Base. By ten o'clock the entire naval base was des-
erted of ships, except for one destroyer and one submarine. So
great was the influx of U.S. Army troops to Key West that the army
requested permission to camp troops at the local baseball stadium.
Some navy wives and children left for their family homes in north-
ern cities, but there was no mass exodus of civilians from the area.

At MacDill Air Force Base near Tampa, military planes were
landing in great numbers. The runways at Patrick Air Force Base
near Cape Canaveral were jammed with more fighter planes than
anyone had seen since World War II. Military trains carrying
troops and shrouded equipment rumbled toward Florida. Realistic
training exercises were organized on Florida's beaches for the newly arriving soldiers. When marines landed at Hollywood Beach,

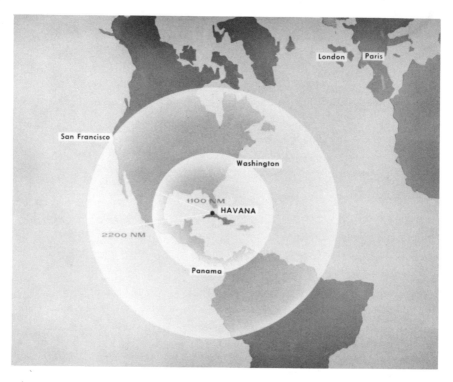

A map showing the striking range from Cuba of MRBMs and IRBMs. Large areas of the Western Hemisphere were in danger.

near Fort Lauderdale, sunbathers quickly mingled with the troops and all semblance of military order disappeared as troops and civilians headed into the nearby bars, hotels, and restaurants. Exercises at more remote sites were more successful.[1]

In Miami the telephones rang constantly at Civil Defense Headquarters. "Where's the nearest fallout shelter?" "What should I do in case of a nuclear attack?" were typical questions. The county manager urged local citizens to tune in their radios and televisions and stock up on canned goods and candles. The state agricultural commissioner said, "We don't want to let hysteria guide our actions." An eleven-year-old girl told her mother, "If we go to war, I could hide under the bed." Her mother replied, "You might have to stay there four or five years!"[2] "Fidel Castro's days are numbered," one Cuban exile in Miami gloated to a reporter. Other Miami residents were equally supportive. "A serious situation, but I feel the president is justified," one said. Another commented, "Mr. Kennedy did as much as he could do short of war. The situation requires as strenuous an effort as he has put forth."

While most people shared those views, many were also shaken by the news. Civil Defense agencies prepared for the worst. "Survival of a direct nuclear hit is impossible," a Civil Defense official gloomily admitted, "but certain precautions will permit survival of radioactive fallout from the blast." Around the country there were spaces in designated fallout shelters in large buildings for about sixty million people. But supplies were scattered and training for necessary personnel almost nonexistent.

In Moscow a visiting American businessman, William Knox, president of Westinghouse International, received a most unlikely and sudden summons to visit Nikita Khrushchev. The Soviet leader was not interested in buying a Westinghouse product; he wanted to use Mr. Knox as a conduit for a private message to President Kennedy. For over three hours Khrushchev spoke his mind to the businessman, who immediately transmitted the first secretary's views to Washington. Khrushchev warned Kennedy that the United States could not take over Cuba. The blockade was an illegal act, he continued, and the Soviet ships heading to Cuba were unarmed. Khrushchev also admitted for the first time that indeed there were nuclear missiles in Cuba totally under Soviet control. They would not be fired unless the United States attacked. The Soviet leader made a point of mentioning that just as United States missiles in Turkey were aimed at the Soviet Union, Soviet missiles in Cuba were aimed at the United States. The message was clear. The United States, like the Soviets, would have to get used to enemy missiles aimed at it. In an ominous move Khrushchev also warned that Soviet submarines were prepared to sink United States ships if Soviet ships were stopped by the quarantine.

Hours before the 10:00 A.M. quarantine deadline, American reconnaissance planes took notice of an unusual event in the mid-Atlantic. Of the nineteen Soviet ships en route to Cuba, sixteen, including five with the large hatches that signified missile cargoes, had slowed down, stopped, or reversed course. Only one, the *Bucharest*, an oil tanker, seemed to be proceeding toward Cuba. With the threat of Russian ships being boarded by Americans, the Soviets thought it prudent to turn back those ships carrying weapons. They did not want the United States closely examining the Soviet Union's latest weapons technology. The Americans did not know it at the time, but one of the ships, the *Poltava*, carried twenty nuclear warheads.

The mood of the ExComm meeting, which began at the exact hour the quarantine went into effect, was tinged with fear. Robert Kennedy referred to that meeting as one of two during the entire crisis that was "the most trying, the most difficult, and the one most filled with tension."[3] What if the ships were only regrouping and then, with submarine escorts, attempted to run through the interdiction line? Indeed, two of the ships were detected only miles away from the line and, more ominously, a Soviet submarine had placed itself between them and the United States ships. The aircraft carrier *Essex* was immediately dispatched to the area with orders to signal the submarine to surface. If it refused, depth charges would be dropped until it did. A misstep would result in war. The president was tense. "His hand went up to his face and covered his mouth. He opened and closed his fist. His face seemed drawn, his eyes pained, almost gray."[4]

"Isn't there some way we can avoid having our first exchange with a Russian submarine—almost anything but that?" the president asked. "No," responded Secretary of Defense McNamara, "there's too much danger to our ships. There is no alternative."[5] At 10:25 the message was received that Soviet ships heading toward the quarantine line had stopped or turned. An immediate order was sent out to the *Essex* not to fire but to allow the Soviet ships every opportunity to turn around. Everyone around the table breathed a sigh of relief. The hidden message was that Khrushchev was not yet prepared to test the blockade and risk expanding the crisis. In perhaps an overly optimistic moment Secretary of State Rusk turned to Secretary McNamara and said, "We're eyeball to eyeball and I think the other fellow just blinked."[6] But the crisis was far from over. Several years later, when he wrote his memoirs, Khrushchev could not bring himself to admit that Soviet ships did not break through the quarantine.

On October 24 the secretary general of the United Nations, U Thant, sent messages to both Kennedy and Khrushchev. He proposed that the Soviets voluntarily stop sending weapons to Cuba and that the United States temporarily lift the quarantine to allow time for a negotiated settlement. Khrushchev immediately accepted the proposal. Kennedy responded with a polite note to the secretary general which in effect said no. Kennedy feared that any delay would result in Soviet completion of the missile sites under construction. The United States position was clear. Not only were new shipments of weapons to be prohibited, but all missile sites in Cuba had to be dismantled and removed before negotiations could begin.

The U.S. military alert, previously raised to DEFCON 3 on October 22, was raised, on October 24, to DEFCON 2, the highest level ever in history and only one level below all-out war. In a most unusual action the signal to U.S. forces around the world was purposely sent uncoded. The commander of the Strategic Air Command (SAC) did this on his own authority to warn the Soviets that the danger of all-out nuclear war was very real.

The undersecretary of state prepared a secret cable for the United States ambassador to Turkey to alert him that thought was being given to the possible exchange of U.S. missiles in Turkey for the Soviet missiles in Cuba. The idea was controversial, but the president was exploring all possibilities to avoid a direct military confrontation.

That evening, October 24, the White House received another letter from Khrushchev. Khrushchev's message was at once demeaning and threatening. The Soviet leader could not forget that the American president was younger than his own son. In his discussion earlier that day with William Knox, Khrushchev alluded to Kennedy's youth as if the president's age somehow diminished his experience and judgment:

You, Mr. President, are not declaring a quarantine, but rather are setting forth an ultimatum and threatening that if we do not give in to your demands you will use force . . . No, Mr. President, I cannot agree to this, and I think that in your own heart you recognize that I am correct. I am convinced that in my place you would act the same way.

Therefore the Soviet Government cannot instruct the captains of Soviet vessels bound for Cuba to observe the orders of American naval forces blockading that Island . . . Naturally we will not simply be bystanders with regard to piratical acts by American ships on the high seas. We will then be forced on our part to take the measures we consider necessary and adequate in order to protect our rights. We have everything necessary to do so.[7]

Early the next morning, October 25, Kennedy's response was sent to Moscow by cable. Khrushchev's letters seemed to have been written in a clearly informal manner, probably by the Soviet leader himself. Kennedy's responses were businesslike and to the point, crafted and amended by the ExComm. In response to Khrushchev's warning, Kennedy stated that the crisis was due to Soviet misrepresentations:

In early September I indicated very plainly that the United States would regard any shipment of offensive weapons as presenting the gravest issues. After that time, this Government received the most explicit assurances from your Government and its representatives . . . that no offensive weapons were being sent to Cuba.

I ask you to recognize clearly, Mr. Chairman, that it was not I who issued the first challenge in this case, and that in the light of this record these activities in Cuba required the responses I have announced.[8]

Since the imposition of the quarantine, several non-Soviet ships had been allowed to cross the interdiction line without inspection. That morning, as the Russian tanker *Bucharest* approached the line, an American warship radioed the ship to identify itself and its cargo. The *Bucharest* promptly replied and identified itself and the cargo of oil. When asked if weapons were aboard, the answer was no. Following instructions from the White House, the *Bucharest* was allowed to proceed to Cuba. The military had originally wanted to board the *Bucharest* to make a point of its authority. But the fact that the ship identified itself to the blockading force satisfied that need. Kennedy did not want to confront the Soviets directly just yet. He was content to allow them more time to analyze the situation.

Meanwhile, in the United States, opinion makers were voicing their own analysis. Walter Lippmann was the most influential journalist of the time. His column was read by decision makers all over the country and especially in Washington. That morning his column attracted more attention than usual. In a clear analysis of the options facing President Kennedy, Lippmann suggested a missile trade between the United States and the Soviet Union:

> *The only place that is truly comparable with Cuba is Turkey. This is the only place where there are strategic weapons right on the frontier of the Soviet Union.*[9]

The Soviets also read Lippmann's column that day and were incorrectly convinced that he was describing *official* United States government policy. Comparisons between Cuba and Turkey had suddenly become popular. The Austrian foreign minister, Bruno Kreisky, also made the same suggestion. But Turkey itself was more reluctant. Responding secretly on October 25 to the American cable sent a day earlier, the Turkish government emphasized the importance of the missiles on its soil "as a symbol of the [NATO] Alliance's determination to use atomic weapons against Russian attack on Turkey."

At the ExComm meeting on the afternoon of October 25 a number of political options were discussed. One of these options proposed sending an impartial South American diplomat to Cuba to convince Castro that the Soviets were merely taking advantage of his country. A plan to drop propaganda leaflets over Cuba was also discussed. At the United Nations, U Thant issued a second appeal to both sides. He again requested the Soviets to keep their ships out of the quarantine area for a limited time and asked the United

States to "do everything possible to avoid a direct confrontation with Soviet ships in the next few days." Kennedy responded, "The existing threat was created by the secret introduction of offensive weapons into Cuba, and the answer lies in the removal of such weapons." He called for the removal of the Soviet weapons and verification that they had actually been dismantled.

To avoid direct conflict with a Soviet-owned ship, the U.S. Navy began shadowing a Lebanese freighter, under Soviet contract, heading toward Cuba. During the night, the *USS Kennedy* radioed the *Marucla* to prepare for boarding the next morning, October 26.

On the afternoon of October 25 millions of Americans watched great drama unfold at the United Nations as Adlai Stevenson forcefully presented the United States case against the Soviet Union. Soviet ambassador Valerian Zorin, that month's president of the council, followed the familiar Soviet script of calling the Americans warmongers and denying the presence of offensive weapons in Cuba. Stevenson responded with biting wit: "This is the first time that I have ever heard it said that the crime is not the burglary but the discovery of the burglar!"

Zorin challenged Stevenson for proof. As the television cameras captured every moment of the debate, Stevenson continued:

> *Well, let me say something to you, Mr. Ambassador: we do have the evidence. We have it, and it is clear and incontrovertible. And let me say something else: these weapons must be taken out of Cuba . . . Do you, Ambassador Zorin, deny that the U.S.S.R. has placed and is placing medium and intermediate range missiles and sites in Cuba? Yes or no? Don't wait for the translation, yes or no?*

The bemused Zorin turned to the American and answered, "I am not in an American courtroom, sir, and therefore I do not wish to answer a question that is put to me in a fashion in which a prosecutor puts questions." Stevenson immediately retorted, "You are in the courtroom of world opinion right now and you can answer yes or no. You have denied that they exist and I want to know whether I have understood you correctly." Zorin replied, "Continue with your statement. You will have your answer in due course."

Stevenson, to laughter in the council chamber, responded with the most remembered line of the entire crisis, "I am prepared to wait for my answer until hell freezes over, if that is your decision." Turning to the easel behind him, Stevenson then added, "And I am also prepared to present the evidence in this room." With that he unveiled enlarged reconnaissance photographs of the missile sites for all to see. The Soviet ambassador had no response.

In Cuba construction at the missile sites proceeded at a feverish pace. The CIA reported to the ExComm that some of the missiles were now ready for launching. Not knowing whether or not they were topped with nuclear warheads, the intelligence agency assumed they were. As the fears escalated, President Kennedy signed an official memorandum authorizing U.S. Air Force planes in Europe to begin carrying nuclear weapons.

Plans also continued for an American invasion of Cuba. The administration itself could not accept Stevenson's invitation to wait "until hell freezes over." Within the next week a decision would have to be made either to expand the blockade or fly air strikes over Cuba, perhaps resulting in a massive military invasion. General Maxwell Taylor, chairman of the Joint Chiefs of Staff, notified the secretary of defense that a full invasion would require at least seven advance days of heavy air strikes to "neutralize or eliminate the hostile air and ground capability."[10] While military planning continued, attention focused on activities in the Caribbean.

EIGHT

DIPLOMATIC OFFENSIVE

❖ ❖ ❖

"War is our enemy and a calamity for all nations."
(NIKITA KHRUSHCHEV)

The *Marucla* was the first ship actually boarded and inspected by the U.S. Navy under the rules of the quarantine established by the United States. Specifically under orders from the president, the navy was not to directly confront a Soviet-owned vessel. The *Marucla*, Lebanese-owned but under charter to the Soviets, was the perfect ship to stop. Two American destroyers, the *USS Pierce* and the *USS Kennedy* (named after the president's older brother, killed in World War II), had been shadowing the freighter during the night of October 25 and maintaining radio contact with its captain. At seven o'clock on the morning of October 26 the *Kennedy* signaled the freighter to stop and prepare for a boarding party. After a cursory inspection, during which no contraband was discovered, the freighter was allowed to continue. As hoped for, no international incident was created and the American right to stop Cuban-bound shipping was not challenged by the Soviets.

In Washington the news was greeted with relief. There was little else to cheer about. Added reconnaissance flights over Cuba, by lower-flying air force planes, revealed new missile sites and in-

United States low altitude reconnaissance airplanes used during the Missile Crisis.

creased construction activity at previously discovered sites. Newspapers continued to speculate about the heavy military buildup, and rumors of an impending American invasion spread to Cuba. So certain was Castro of an immediate invasion that he went to the Soviet embassy in Havana and spent the night in the embassy's underground bomb shelter. From the embassy's secure basement he sent a secret message to Khrushchev, imploring the Soviets to unleash a preemptive nuclear strike at the United States. Castro also ordered his own forces to open fire on any American aircraft flying over Cuban territory.

Khrushchev later said in his memoirs, "It became clear to us that Fidel totally failed to understand our purpose. . . . We had installed the missiles not for the purpose of attacking the United States, but to keep the United States from attacking Cuba."[1]

President Kennedy, not at all optimistic, glumly told the Ex-Comm group on October 26, that "We will get the Soviet strategic missiles out of Cuba only by invading Cuba or trading." He doubted that the quarantine alone would produce a withdrawal of the weapons. Others spoke of the inevitability of air strikes to eliminate the missiles. The president ordered the State Department to begin planning the establishment of a new government in Cuba should an invasion be undertaken. Secretary McNamara estimated that an invasion would result in a heavy toll in American casualties. Military experts later estimated that within the first ten days of such an invasion there would be over eighteen thousand American casualties.[2]

Plans were made to approach Castro personally through the good offices of a friendly South American ambassador to Cuba. The ambassador would be instructed to warn Castro that the Soviet Union had "placed the future of the Castro regime and the well-being of the Cuban people in great jeopardy."[3] In the end, the plan was never put into effect. The president did not think Castro would be impressed.

At the White House plans were finalized for an evacuation of key governmental personnel and their families if Washington came under nuclear attack. Special passes were distributed and an assembly area was designated at the Reno Reservoir in northwest Washington, where a motorcade would be formed to transport people to the relocation area. Individuals on the list were told "minimal supplies of food and water will be included in the planning, so that it will not be necessary for dependents to bring any additional equipment."[4] The president himself did not consider leaving Washington.

John Scali, a respected ABC News diplomatic correspondent, was having a busy day, as were most Washington reporters. Too busy to leave the State Department pressroom, he had just gulped down a sandwich when his telephone rang. An acquaintance, Alexander Fomin, counselor at the Soviet embassy, wanted to meet him for lunch right away. Despite Scali's busy schedule (and the fact that he already had eaten), the reporter agreed to meet the insistent Fomin at the nearby Occidental Restaurant in ten minutes. For despite Fomin's official embassy title, it was correctly assumed in Washington that he was, in fact, a high-ranking Soviet intelligence officer. Scali was curious.

At the restaurant Fomin greeted Scali with the ominous words "War seems about to break out." Once the waiter had taken their order, the visibly nervous Fomin blurted out a startling set of terms to Scali for ending the missile crisis. First, the missile sites in Cuba would be dismantled and shipped back to the Soviet Union under United Nations supervision. Second, the Soviets would send no further shipments of offensive weapons to Cuba. Third, the United States would have to pledge not to invade Cuba. Fomin further suggested that if these steps were brought up by Ambassador Stevenson at the United Nations, the Soviet ambassador would be receptive. Fomin then took the unusual step of giving his home telephone number to the reporter and urged Scali to take the matter up at once with the State Department.

Now it was Scali's turn to be nervous. Racing back to the State Department, he headed directly to the office of Roger Hilsman, the Director of Intelligence, and dictated an account of his strange meeting.[5] To the experts at the State Department, this seemed to be a desperate act by Khrushchev to avoid war. They were never certain that the message came directly from the Soviet leader. Nonetheless, Hilsman rushed Scali down to Dean Rusk's office and had him relate the story of his meeting to the secretary of state.

Rusk drafted a short response on a piece of lined yellow paper and after checking it out with the White House gave the paper to Scali with instructions to relay the message to Fomin. Scali called Fomin and they arranged to meet at 7:35 that evening, October 26. In the coffee shop of the Statler Hotel, Scali recited the message from Rusk:

I have reason to believe that the USG [United States Government] sees real possibilities in this and supposes that representatives of the two governments could work this matter out with U Thant and with each other. My impression is, however, that time is very urgent.[6]

Fomin then asked if the message came from the highest authority in the United States. Scali's answer was yes. Fomin said he would immediately relay the message to the highest authority in the Soviet Union and rushed off into the night. By the time Scali returned to the State Department, just before nine o'clock, the experts there were in the process of receiving a rambling, sometimes disjointed message from Khrushchev to Kennedy. It had been received hours earlier at the Moscow embassy and as quickly as it was translated into English by the embassy staff, it was being transmitted by teletype in four parts to Washington. Because of the poor communications links, it took nearly seven hours for the entire message to reach Washington. As each part was received, it was minutely examined and evaluated. Elie Abel, in his book *The Missile Crisis*, said that the letter "read like the nightmare outcry of a frightened man."

Khrushchev began by saying that each side had already made its position on the crisis quite clear to the other. Speaking out about the dangers of war to all peoples, he said, "War is our enemy and a calamity for all nations." He alluded to both his and Kennedy's experiences with war. "I know," he continued, "that war ends only when it has rolled through cities and villages, sowing death and destruction everywhere."

The tone and language of the letter was conciliatory and revealed a man who seemed not ready to launch a third world war: "Only lunatics or suicides, who themselves want to perish and before they die destroy the world, could do this. But we want to live and by no means do we want to destroy your country." Then he all but admitted what the United States had been saying, "I do not mean to say that there have been no shipments of armaments at all. No, there were such shipments." Khrushchev also agreed to accept the U Thant proposal of temporarily keeping Soviet ships away from the quarantine line in return for a United States agreement not to confront Soviet ships during negotiations: "This would be a way out of the situation which has evolved that would give nations a chance to breathe easily."

Such a temporary freeze would not, however, remove the missiles already in Cuba. Sensing this would not be acceptable to the Americans, Khrushchev finally came to the nub of his proposal:

If the President and Government of the United States would give their assurances that the United States would itself not take part in an attack upon Cuba and would restrain others from such action; if you recall your Navy—this would immediately change everything.

Let us therefore display statesmanlike wisdom. I propose: we, for our part, will declare that our ships bound for Cuba are not carrying any armaments. You will declare that the United States will not invade Cuba with its troops and will not support any other forces which might intend to invade Cuba. Then the necessity for the presence of our military specialists in Cuba will be obviated.[7]

In short, Khrushchev proposed an end to the crisis by agreeing to remove the missiles in exchange for a U.S. guarantee not to invade Cuba. The timing of the Khrushchev letter indicated that it was written before the first Fomin meeting even took place.

The unusual meetings between Scali and Fomin, and the arrival of the Khrushchev letter perplexed the ExComm members. As the ExComm reconvened that Friday night, October 26, the members debated the meaning of the Khrushchev letter and its relationship, if any, to the Fomin message. Taken together, both formed the basis for a mutual agreement to ending the crisis. The major difference was Fomin's involvement of the United Nations to monitor the Soviet removal of weapons.

For the ExComm members the message from Khrushchev seemed like a breath of fresh air. They had gone without sleep for days, had eaten sandwiches and cold meals at their desks, and had been under constant emotional pressure. They had all become irritable, and none could bear the pressure much longer. The president decided to wait for the next day, after the Khrushchev letter could be carefully studied, to send the Soviets his response.

Meanwhile, without informing the ExComm, the president sent his brother on a secret mission. Late Friday night, October 26, the attorney general of the United States hurried through a back door of the Soviet embassy to meet again with Ambassador Dobrynin. The ambassador began by repeating the usual Soviet views and criticized Kennedy for constantly referring to the "security of the U.S." The ambassador then asked if the United States didn't have missiles in Turkey that threatened the security of the Soviet Union. According to Dobrynin, Kennedy then left the room to call the president. Upon his return he told Dobrynin that the United States was now ready to explore the question of missiles in Turkey. The ambassador then asked for assurances that the United States would not attack Cuba. Kennedy left the room again to call his brother and returned, saying, "This can be discussed in a positive way."

The hope generated by Khrushchev's October 26th letter did not last long. The next morning, October 27, during the ten o'clock Ex-Comm meeting, a second Khrushchev letter to Kennedy began arriving. Unlike the first letter, which was transmitted privately, the new letter was broadcast directly over Radio Moscow's shortwave service for all to hear. Khrushchev was under pressure from his own military advisers, who did not agree with his original decision to reach a peaceful accord with the Americans. In his memoirs Khrushchev remembered what happened: "They looked at me as though I was out of my mind or, what was worse, a traitor . . . what good would it have done me in the last hour of my life to know that though our great nation and the United States were in complete ruins, the national honor of the Soviet Union was intact?"[8]

Khrushchev's second letter was much more polished and organized than the first. It bore the mark of having been carefully composed and edited. As the ExComm members received the ongoing translation, it became painfully clear that something new and dramatic had been added to Khrushchev's original proposal—Turkey. The assembled members were stunned by the new tone and the content. What had happened to make Khrushchev choose a new tactic? Some thought Khrushchev might have been toppled from power by hard-liners in the Kremlin and that the hard-liners were the authors of this second letter. Something dramatic must have happened to result in the sudden injection of Turkish missiles into the confrontation equation. After Robert Kennedy's secret meeting the previous night, the new subject of Turkish missiles could not have been much of a surprise to the president, however. The president had said nothing of the Dobrynin visit to his advisers. Indeed, several passages of the new letter were reminiscent of the conversation between Dobrynin and Robert Kennedy:

> *You wish to ensure the security of your country, and this is understandable. But Cuba, too, wants the same thing; all countries want to maintain their security. But how are we, the Soviet Union, our Government, to assess your actions which are expressed in the fact that you have surrounded the Soviet Union with military bases . . . Your missiles are located in Britain, are located in Italy, and are aimed against us. Your missiles are located in Turkey.*

> *You are disturbed over Cuba. You say that this disturbs you because it is 90 miles by sea from the coast of the United States of America. But Turkey adjoins us . . .*

> *I therefore make this proposal: we are willing to remove from Cuba the means which you regard as offensive. We are willing to carry this out and to make this pledge in the United Nations. Your representatives will make a declaration to the effect that the United States, for its part, considering the uneasiness and anxiety of the Soviet State, will remove its analogous means from Turkey.*

There it was. An offer for an even exchange. The missiles in Cuba for the missiles in Turkey. For nearly two weeks the ExComm had consciously attempted to prevent any link between the secret buildup of Soviet missiles in Cuba and the public placement of American missiles in NATO countries. But for President Kennedy the debate had gone on far too long. It was time for both sides to make concessions and end the danger. Although the solution was in sight, the events that unfolded that Saturday, October 27, would bring Kennedy and Khrushchev closer to the disaster each wished so desperately to avoid.

NINE

BLACK SATURDAY

❖ ❖ ❖

"I thought I might never see another Saturday night."
(ROBERT MCNAMARA)

Through all the years of the cold war, the FBI maintained a close watch on Communist bloc diplomats in the United States. A report from New York early Saturday, October 27, indicated that Soviet officials were preparing to burn secret files at their United Nations Mission and at their residence compound on Long Island. Such extreme action usually signified a break in diplomatic relations and an imminent state of war.

That Saturday was not a good day in Washington. Even before the ExComm began its 10:00 A.M. meeting, bad news had been piling up. An early morning CIA report announced that although no new Cuban missile sites had been identified, a number of the known medium-range missile sites were now fully operational. The Cubans, still expecting a momentary American invasion, continued to mobilize their troops and defenses. In addition, a report from the Caribbean indicated that a Soviet tanker, the *Grozny*, seemed to be ignoring the temporary freeze agreed to by both sides and was steaming steadily toward the quarantine line.

As the ExComm members discussed what action to take if the tanker actually crossed the line, a report was received that sent chills through those in the room. An American U-2, flying over Alaska to collect air-data samples, accidently strayed over Soviet territory into Siberia. To avoid possible misunderstanding during the crisis, the United States had forbidden all spy flights over Soviet territory. As Soviet fighters rose to intercept it, American fighters, armed with nuclear-tipped air-to-air missiles, entered Soviet air space and escorted the American spy plane back to safety. "This means war with the Soviet Union," McNamara screamed. The president was less emotional and brushed the situation off by saying, "There's always some [one] who doesn't get the word."

Before the ExComm members could return to their discussion, Khrushchev's October 27 message linking Cuba to Turkey began arriving. Douglas Dillon later remarked that the ExComm reacted to the second letter "like a bucket of ice in the face."[1] Just as the officials began analyzing the letter, another ominous report arrived, escalating the crisis even further. A U-2 had been shot down over Cuba by a Soviet SAM missile and the pilot, Major Rudolph Anderson, was missing and presumed dead. Anderson, ironically, was one of the two original U-2 pilots whose flights discovered the offensive missile sites.

Soviet leaders in Moscow were just as surprised at the downing of the U-2 as the Americans. A Soviet commander at a missile site near Banes on Cuba's north coast ignored a rule that required advance permission from Moscow to fire at an American plane. On his own he issued the order to bring down the spy plane. Other non-U-2 reconnaissance flights reported they were being shot at by small arms and antiaircraft batteries presumably under Cuban control.

Earlier in the week the ExComm decided that if any American U-2 planes were shot down over Cuba the responsible SAM missile site would be destroyed. Now that a plane had actually been downed and its pilot killed, the military assumed that the first air strike of the crisis was about to take place. The Pentagon made ready to execute the order as soon as it arrived. The chairman of the Joint Chiefs of Staff, Maxwell Taylor, urged that a massive air strike against missile sites in Cuba should begin no later than Monday morning, October 29. The ExComm was not quite that

At an ExComm meeting, Vice President Lyndon Johnson and Attorney General Robert Kennedy are shown planning.

ready to escalate the crisis, however. They anticipated the resulting Soviet retaliation.

Patience was wearing thin and time was drawing near for action. As the ExComm members continued to debate what to do about the missiles in Turkey, Secretary McNamara told his colleagues:

> *We must be in a position to attack, quickly. We've been fired on today. We're going to send surveillance aircraft in tomorrow. Those are going to be fired on without question. We're going to respond. You can't do this [limited escalation] very long . . . So we must be prepared to attack Cuba quickly . . . I personally believe that this is almost certain to lead to an invasion.*[2]

The president also realized that the debate could not continue forever. That morning's U-2 events clearly illustrated the dangers of unexpected happenings. Kennedy suggested that "if we don't get some satisfaction from the Russians or U Thant or Cuba tomorrow night, figure that Monday we're going to do something about the SAM sites."[3]

The president sent a special message to U Thant at the United Nations:

> *A number of proposals have been made to you and to the United States in the last thirty-six hours. I would appreciate your urgently ascertaining whether the Soviet Union is willing immediately to cease work on these bases in Cuba and render the weapons inoperable under UN verification so that various solutions can be discussed.*[4]

In spite of these alarming events, the ExComm returned to an analysis of Khrushchev's second letter. The members tried to understand why the Soviets had suddenly increased their demands. Some thought hard-liners in the Kremlin might have disapproved of Khrushchev's private letter to Kennedy and decided to exert more pressure on the United States. Some thought Khrushchev might have been misled by incorrectly thinking the Walter Lippmann article, which mentioned a trade of Turkish missiles for Cuban missiles, was crafted by the Kennedy administration. As they discussed possibilities, Kennedy still did not mention the secret overture by Robert Kennedy to Dobrynin of the previous evening, October 26. The president pushed for a quick response to Khrushchev's original letter but at the same time favored discussing the Turkish missile option with NATO as a fallback position.

During the ExComm deliberations on October 27, Kennedy kept subtly pushing for a Cuban-Turkish missile trade. "He's [Khrushchev's] got us in a pretty good spot here, because most people will regard this as not an unreasonable proposal, I'll just tell you that. In fact, in many ways . . ." McGeorge Bundy rudely interrupted the president to ask, "But what most people, Mr. President?" To which Kennedy responded, "I think you're going to find it very difficult to explain why we are going to take hostile military action in Cuba, against these sites—what we've been thinking about—the thing that he's saying is, 'If you'll get yours out of Turkey, we'll get ours out of Cuba.' I think we've got a very tough one here." Kennedy then instructed some of his aides to work further on a scenario for removing the missiles from Turkey and to report back to the Ex-Comm at a 9:00 P.M. meeting.

The problem of the Turkish missiles was defined by the State Department's Roger Hilsman in political and material terms. American allies would view the removal of missiles from Turkey as "an indication that the U.S. would not stand up to Soviet threats elsewhere, particularly in Berlin." He predicted that the removal of the missiles would "have repercussions in other parts of the Middle East . . . as a confession of U.S. weakness."

The Kennedy administration had earlier discounted the military value of the Turkish missiles, which by 1962 were outmoded and vulnerable to Soviet attack. Hilsman reinforced that view: "The Soviet missiles in Cuba on the other hand are a highly significant addition to Soviet missile strength capable of reaching U.S. targets. . . . On balance, therefore, such an agreement [as presented by Khrushchev] might be considered to be to the net military advantage of the U.S.—we would have exchanged a small increment of our strength for a much larger portion of Soviet strength."[5]

During the lunch break, Secretary Rusk called John Scali to his office. Rusk informed the journalist of the changes that had taken place by the introduction of the Turkish missiles to the crisis solution. He also showed Scali the latest air reconnaissance photos from Cuba of operational Soviet missiles. Rusk wanted Scali to meet Alexander Fomin once more to ascertain just what had gone wrong with the original plan presented by Fomin at the restaurant meeting and to impress on him the gravity of the situation.

Perhaps it was his television background, or just the feeling he had been duped, but John Scali was livid when he saw Fomin again. As they faced each other in an empty ballroom of the Statler Hotel, Scali exploded. Demanding to know why Khrushchev had done a "flip-flop," Scali accused Fomin of arranging a "stinking doublecross." The Soviet agent was speechless as Scali continued, "I don't care . . . whether it was Walter Lippmann or Cleopatra. That offer [presented in the second Khrushchev letter] is totally unacceptable—now, tomorrow and ad infinitum." Fomin recovered enough to mumble "don't get excited" and informed Scali that as far as he knew the first proposal was still on the table. Scali told him of

the Soviet downing of the U-2 and then exploded again: "If you
think the United States is bluffing, you are part of the most colos-
sal misjudgment of American intentions in history. We are absolutely determined to get those missiles out of there." Then, perhaps
carried away by the intensity of the moment, he added a warning
he had no right making but which greatly impressed his listener:
"American invasion of Cuba is only hours away."[6] With Scali's
words fresh in his mind, Fomin rushed back to his embassy to relay
the startling information to Moscow. Scali reported on the meeting
to the ExComm and conveyed his feeling that Fomin knew nothing
of Khrushchev's new set of conditions.

Faced with the two Khrushchev letters, the ExComm continued
to thrash out possible responses. The debate was often confusing
and angry. It was clear that the Soviet demand for the removal of
the Turkish missiles had less to do with Turkey than it did with
NATO. A United States pullout of the missiles from Turkey would
weaken the Western alliance and benefit the Soviet Union and the
Warsaw Pact. As the debate dragged on, an idea began to emerge to
respond to the first Khrushchev letter without acknowledging re-
ceipt of the second. Some thought the ruse might work. The president agreed to issue such a letter, but he was not confident that
Khrushchev would accept it. A response was drafted by Robert
Kennedy and Ted Sorensen and edited by the rest of the ExComm.
As stated in his response, the president basically accepted the
suggestions of Khrushchev's October 26th letter.

To at least acknowledge the second letter, Kennedy agreed that
once the Cuban crisis was settled they could "work toward a more
general arrangement regarding 'other armaments,' as proposed in
your second letter which you made public." "But," the president
emphasized, "the first thing that needs to be done . . . is for work to
cease on offensive missile bases in Cuba and for all weapons systems in Cuba capable of offensive use to be rendered inoperable
under effective United Nations arrangements."[7]

The president then repeated the basic components as suggested
by Khrushchev in the first letter of October 26. The Soviets would
remove all weapons from Cuba under UN supervision in return for
American lifting of the quarantine and, as Kennedy put it, giving

"assurances against an invasion of Cuba." He closed the letter by again linking himself with the Soviet leader. ". . . I hope we can quickly agree along the lines outlined in this letter and in your letter of October 26."

Kennedy decided to issue the response directly to the press to avoid communication delays, as Khrushchev had done with his second letter. When the ExComm meeting ended, Kennedy invited Secretary of Defense McNamara, Robert Kennedy, McGeorge Bundy, Secretary of State Rusk, Ambassador Thompson, and Ted Sorensen into his office. He was concerned that the letter alone might not be enough to convince Khrushchev. He then informed this smaller group of advisers about his brother's conversation on the night of October 26 with Ambassador Dobrynin and told them not to reveal that information to the other ExComm members. The group decided that the attorney general should contact Dobrynin again to warn him that the end was fast approaching and failure of the Soviet Union to accept the terms of this letter would result in military action against Cuba. Dean Rusk further suggested that Robert Kennedy inform the ambassador that the United States would pull the missiles from Turkey within a few months but that news must not be made public.

At 7:45 that evening, October 27, Ambassador Dobrynin arrived at Robert Kennedy's office in the Justice Department. The attorney general handed him a copy of the letter sent to Khrushchev. Kennedy reminded him that the situation was getting more dangerous. There was increasing danger of additional U-2 flights being shot down, with the consequence of American military response. Dobrynin responded that the Cubans "resented the fact that [the U.S. was] violating Cuban air space." Kennedy answered that "if we had not violated Cuban air space, we would still be believing what Khrushchev had said . . ."[8]

"If you do not remove those bases," Kennedy warned, "we would remove them." He told the ambassador that a Soviet commitment was needed "by tomorrow." In a top-secret memorandum of the meeting to the secretary of state, Kennedy later wrote that he told Dobrynin that while the Soviet Union "might take retaliatory action . . . he should understand that before this was over, while there might be dead Americans there would also be dead Russians."[9]

When Dobrynin raised the question of Turkish missiles, Robert Kennedy told him "no deal of this kind could be made." But he added an off-the-record assurance: "President Kennedy had been anxious to remove those missiles from Turkey and Italy for a long time . . . and it was our judgment that, within a short time after this crisis was over, those missiles would be gone."[10] But a clear warning was also given that "the understanding would be cancelled at once if the Soviets tried to claim public credit for removing the Turkish missiles." As the meeting with Dobrynin ended, Robert Kennedy again repeated that "this matter could not wait and that he had better contact Mr. Khrushchev and have a commitment from him by the next day to withdraw the missile bases under United Nations supervision for otherwise . . . there would be drastic consequences."[11] Dobrynin hurried back to the embassy, called for a bicycle-riding Western Union messenger and, hoping it would get there in time, sent word of his meeting with Robert Kennedy back to Moscow.

At 9:00 P.M., with the message for Khrushchev on its way to Moscow, the exhausted ExComm reconvened once again in the White House. Expecting a rejection by Khrushchev of Kennedy's demands, the members discussed the next steps that needed to be taken. The president activated twenty-four air force reserve squadrons of fourteen thousand troops. He was also prepared to mobilize American private shipping the next day, if necessary. He also directed Ambassador Stevenson to inform U Thant that the Soviet tanker, *Grozny,* was still approaching the quarantine line in spite of Soviet assurances that the interdiction line would not be crossed. If it became necessary to fire upon the *Grozny,* the possibility existed that the Soviets could retaliate. Robert Kennedy later said his brother "had not abandoned hope, but what hope there was now rested with Khrushchev's revising his course within the next few hours. It was a hope, not an expectation. The expectation was a military confrontation by Tuesday and possibly tomorrow . . ."[12]

The ExComm then finalized plans for air strikes on the Cuban missile sites and for a tightening of the quarantine to include all

President Kennedy with Secretary of State Dean Rusk.

petroleum imports into Cuba. The lack of oil would force Cuba's industries to shut down quickly and would severely hinder all transportation and electricity on the island. Turning to the Attorney General, Secretary McNamara said, "I think . . . we need to have two things ready, a government for Cuba, because we're going to need one and secondly, plans for how to respond to the Soviet Union in Europe, because sure as hell they're going to do something there." From another part of the room someone tried to lower the tension and joked, "Suppose we make Bobby mayor of Havana."[13] As the men headed out the door, the president could only say, "Now it can go either way."

Late that evening, October 27, the president and Secretary of State Rusk took one additional secret step without informing anyone else. They feared that Khrushchev would not accept the private assurances of trading Turkish and Cuban missiles. The impasse might result in war. Rusk telephoned an old friend in New York, Andrew Cordier, president of Columbia University. Rusk dictated a statement to the surprised Cordier, instructing him to deliver it personally to U Thant at the United Nations if and when directed to do so by Rusk. The statement was a public announcement of a United Nations solution to the crisis, urging the United States to remove its missiles from Turkey and the Soviet Union to remove its missiles from Cuba simultaneously. The understanding was that Kennedy would then immediately agree to the terms, previously agreed to by Khrushchev, thereby ending the crisis.

In Moscow and Washington the night of October 27 was filled with fear and tension. Robert McNamara later said, "I thought I might never see another Saturday night."[14] In Moscow some members of the Communist Central Committee began moving their families out of the city.

The next morning, Sunday, October 28, a message from Khrushchev was broadcast on Radio Moscow for President Kennedy:

Esteemed Mr. President:

I have received your message of October 27, 1962. I express my satisfaction and gratitude for the sense of proportion and understanding of the responsibility borne by you at present for the preservation of peace throughout the world . . .

In order to complete with greater speed the liquidation of the conflict . . . the Soviet Government . . . in addition to previously issued instructions on the cessation of further work at building sites for the weapons, has issued a new order on the dismantling of the weapons which you describe as "offensive," and their crating and return to the Soviet Union.

Without waiting for the official letter to arrive, Kennedy penned an immediate response to Khrushchev, which was broadcast over the Voice of America:

I think that you and I, with our heavy responsibilities for the maintenance of peace, were aware that developments were approaching a point where events could have become unmanageable. So I welcome this message and consider it an important contribution to peace.

Suddenly and without fanfare the crisis was over. Not everyone was satisfied with the conclusion of the tension. In Havana, Fidel Castro's anger was uncontrollable. In his view, his friends, the Soviets, had betrayed him. He saw the withdrawal of the missiles as a dangerous capitulation to the United States, which could yet end with the invasion of his country. In an unprecedented show of force, Castro ordered Cuban troops to surround the Soviet missile sites. Only with the intervention of a Soviet envoy, quickly dispatched to Cuba, was the confrontation halted and the dismantling of the sites begun.

In Washington several military leaders were upset with their commander in chief. Admiral Anderson complained, "We have been had." General Curtis LeMay, the tough-talking air force head, suggested that the United States go into Cuba "and make a strike on Monday anyway." What American military leaders did not know was that the outnumbered Soviet troops in Cuba had orders to use tactical nuclear weapons against American invaders. An invasion of Cuba would have been disastrous for the Americans and would have automatically escalated the scale of destruction.

The scheduled 11:00 A.M. ExComm meeting on Sunday morning was the most relaxed to date. Secretary McNamara announced that the Soviet tanker, *Grozny*, was standing still in the water and no other Soviet ships were approaching the quarantine zone. In response the president halted the flight of reconnaissance planes over Cuba for that day. Kennedy urged all those present to be cautious with their comments to the press. "Although we welcome Khrushchev's reply, we are under no illusions nor can we reach any general conclusions about how the Russians will act in the future in areas other than Cuba. Khrushchev's decision has to be implemented and many serious problems will be encountered in the withdrawal of Soviet weapons from Cuba."[15]

Negotiations began with the Soviets over the removal of the of-

The same U-2 photography which discovered the offensive missile sites in Cuba also revealed them being dismantled.

fensive weapons. By November 7, 1962, the CIA reported that crated missiles were heading back to the Soviet Union by ship and that missile sites throughout Cuba were being dismantled and bulldozed. The removal of the outmoded Soviet IL-28 bombers remained a stumbling block for a few weeks longer, but they also were eventually removed after another series of letters between Khrushchev and Kennedy. Once the question of the bombers was resolved, the United States formally lifted the quarantine around Cuba on November 21, 1962. The military's DEFCON status was raised back to 4—the "normal" cold war status.

TEN

STEPPING BACK FROM DANGER

❖ ❖ ❖

"You accuse me of pulling out our missiles. What do you mean,
that we should have started a world war over them?"
(NIKITA KHRUSHCHEV TO THE SOVIET PRESIDIUM)

W ho won? The clear winner was the human race. In a speech given in December 1962 Nikita Khrushchev proclaimed that "it was sanity, the cause of peace and security of peoples, that won." John F. Kennedy, unwilling to gloat over his country's success, preferred instead to speak about the danger of confrontation in the nuclear age: "When you look at all those misjudgments which brought on war, and then you see the Soviet Union and the United States, so far separated in their beliefs . . . and you put the nuclear equation into that struggle; that is what makes this . . . such a dangerous time. . . . One mistake can make this whole thing blow up."[1]

Following the failure of the Bay of Pigs invasion and the continuing struggle over Berlin, the United States emerged from the Cuban Missile Crisis with greater prestige worldwide. Kennedy and the Democrats proved they were not "soft on Communism." For the Soviet Union the crisis was an acute embarrassment.

To the Cubans the event that nearly plunged the world into war is known as the October Crisis. The Cubans were grateful to the

Soviet Union for coming to their defense at a time when it seemed almost certain to them that the United States was about to invade. Although they successfully repulsed the Bay of Pigs invasion, the Cubans were aware of the constant United States threats to overthrow the Communist government of Fidel Castro. Thirty years later Castro told a conference, "We didn't like the missiles. If it had been a question of our defense, we wouldn't have accepted them. . . . We looked at it from the point of view of our moral, political and internationalist duty." Yet, when the Soviets removed the offensive missiles, the Cubans felt abandoned. Castro sent Khrushchev an emotional message, urging the Soviets to rain nuclear missiles upon the United States. The Soviet leader dismissed that plea. "He [Castro] was a young hotheaded man, so he thought we were retreating and capitulating. He did not understand our action was necessary to prevent a military confrontation."[2]

The Soviets refer to the events of October 1962 as the Caribbean Crisis. What led Khrushchev to embark on this adventure? First, he was painfully aware that his country was overmatched in technical superiority and nuclear weapons capability (five thousand intercontinental warheads for the Americans and only three hundred for the Soviets). During a visit to Bulgaria early in 1962, he stared across the expanse of the Black Sea. He knew that beyond the horizon, in Turkey, United States missiles stood ready to be fired at targets in the Soviet Union. By placing offensive missiles in Cuba, right next to the United States, Khrushchev "could teach the Americans a lesson" and compensate for his own country's missile inferiority. Only later did Khrushchev make a startling admission: "To tell the truth, I have to say that if the Americans had started a war . . . we were not prepared to adequately attack the United States. In that case, we would have been forced to start a war in Europe. Then, of course, a world war would have begun."[3]

Second, the Cubans had turned to him for help. The Bay of Pigs invasion convinced both Cuba and the Soviet Union that the United States would imminently invade the island. Continuing American military exercises around the Caribbean only heightened their belief. When John Kennedy "gave assurances" to Khrushchev against a United States invasion of Cuba, it was not the same as an iron-clad, signed guarantee. The United States wanted to keep its options open. Nonetheless, United States troops never invaded.

Additionally, in planning for the secret placement of the missiles in Cuba, Khrushchev never considered an American response. When the American U-2 discovered the missile sites, the Soviets tried to deny their presence. The proof of the photographs was overwhelming, however. So sure were the Soviets in Cuba that spy flights would never detect the construction that they did not even order their troops to camouflage the missile sites. The deception nearly worked. Because of weather conditions, the United States had to suspend U-2 flights for a time. Had they waited much longer, the missiles in Cuba would have been ready to fire.

Lastly, Khrushchev underestimated Kennedy's convictions. After meeting President Kennedy in Berlin in 1961, Khrushchev formed the opinion that the young American leader was "not strong enough"—a perfect candidate for Khrushchev's legendary boorish intimidation. Khrushchev was wrong.

To the rest of the world those fateful weeks in 1962 are known as the Cuban Missile Crisis. The United States was skillfully lulled into a false sense of security by Khrushchev's assurances that no offensive missiles would ever be placed in Cuba. When American reconnaissance flights ultimately discovered the truth, Kennedy was angered by the deception and resolved to remove those missiles no matter what the cost.

The fact that the crisis ended without war is largely due to two factors—fear of nuclear annihilation and simple luck. Neither superpower leader wanted to be responsible for bringing an end to civilization, so both were extremely guarded in their actions. The unspoken factors throughout those trying weeks were miscalculations and faulty analysis on both sides. ExComm member McGeorge Bundy stated the situation in these words, "We won the battle of the blunders."

While the U-2s were ultimately responsible for uncovering the

John F. Kennedy in the Oval Office. In spite of the hard work of the Ex-Comm and the advice of others within the government, the ultimate decision rested on one person, the President of the United States.

Soviet plans, other intelligence was either wrong or misleading, thus increasing the chance for blunders. American intelligence indicated that there were no more than ten thousand Soviet troops in Cuba. They were chagrined to learn later that the number was over 40,000. Likewise, the number of Cuban troops mobilized was also greatly underestimated. The CIA reported at the time of the crisis that there were no nuclear warheads in Cuba. Later disclosure by the Soviets indicated that there were thirty-six such warheads on the island, although none had yet been mounted onto the missiles. More frightening was the fact that Soviet troops in Cuba were armed with nuclear tactical weapons and permission from Moscow to use them against an invading American army. Had President Kennedy accepted the strong advice of his military leaders to invade Cuba, American troops would have come under local nuclear attack, which could have quickly escalated into a global confrontation with the Soviets.

For his part, Kennedy showed extreme coolness and fortitude under pressure. As a young, relatively inexperienced leader, he resisted the advice of the generals and tried to restrain their professional tendency to react militarily. Sorensen credited the successful outcome of the crisis to "a carefully balanced and precisely measured combination of defense, diplomacy, and dialogue."[4] Secretary of Defense McNamara recounted that "our quarantine was intended to be a political signal, not a textbook military operation, and trying to get that across to the military caused us all a lot of headaches. For twelve days I lived in the Pentagon, from the 16th to the 27th, because I feared that they might not understand that this was a communications exercise, not a military operation."[5]

Yet even that attempt to carefully monitor the military was not completely foolproof. The raising of the U.S. military alert status to DEFCON 2, the highest level ever, was done in "the clear" by a general without approval from the president or secretary of defense. The resulting heightening of tensions in Moscow did nothing to calm war fears.

When President Kennedy made his October 1962 speech, in ef-

fect drawing a line in the sand over which the Soviets must not
pass, he referred directly to "offensive missiles." Ted Sorensen said,
"I believe the President drew the line precisely where he thought
the Soviets were not and would not be: that is to say, if we had
known that the Soviets were putting forty missiles in Cuba we
might . . . have drawn the line at one hundred . . . we simply
thought the Soviets weren't going to deploy any there anyway."[6]

When Secretary McNamara said "You can't anticipate all the details of any operation," he spoke for both sides. The two downed U-2
planes serve as good illustrations. When the American spy plane
accidently overflew Soviet territory, the incident could easily have
escalated into a shooting war between the two sides. The American
planes that entered Soviet airspace to escort the U-2 to safety were
armed with nuclear air-to-air missiles. Should one of them have
been fired, the Soviets would have surely retaliated.

When Major Anderson's U-2 was shot down over Cuba, it was
due to the direct orders of local Soviet officers who bypassed Moscow for permission. This indicated that accidents and miscalculations were not limited to one side. The two U-2 incidents sobered
both Kennedy and Khrushchev's thinking about their options. Neither leader wanted a war, yet each pushed the other to the limit.
While Khrushchev was sending Kennedy messages of peace, Soviet
troops in Cuba were under orders to speed up completion of the
launch sites and make the missiles ready for firing. Even as the
United States imposed the quarantine around Cuba, Khrushchev
was telling his captains to ram on through. He quickly changed his
orders, however, and ordered the "large hatch" ships—the ones carrying missiles and warheads—to turn back. He did not want their
cargoes searched or seized by the Americans.

The crisis provided an important lasting legacy to both sides. It
demonstrated the fragility of superpower strategies in a nuclear
age. Since neither side was willing to cross the "nuclear threshold"
to make a political point, it opened opportunities to debate ratio-
nally the important issues that divided both. President Kennedy
presented his foreign policy goals in a speech at American University in Washington in June 1963:

*And if we cannot now end our differences, at least we can help
make the world safe for diversity. For in the final analysis our
most basic common link is that we all inhabit this planet. We all
breathe the same air. We all cherish our children's future. And we
are all mortal.*[7]

Kennedy spoke prophetically about mortality. Five months after
delivering those words, he was killed by an assassin's bullet.

What resulted from the Cuban Missile Crisis? Primarily, some
first steps were taken to reduce the dangers inherent in a continuing cold war. In 1963 the United States, the Soviet Union, and
Great Britain signed a Limited Nuclear Test Ban Treaty to eliminate atmospheric, underwater, and outer-space testing of nuclear
weapons. A special "hotline" was established between Washington
and Moscow to allow for instant communications between both
country's leaders. During the Missile Crisis, seven-hour delays for
messages to reach Washington and the reliance on bicycle-riding
Western Union messengers were unacceptable means of communication in a nuclear age.

Berlin, although a sensitive spot for decades to follow, ceased being a potential military flash point. The members of NATO were
impressed by the commitment Kennedy made not to weaken the
alliance. (They did not know at the time of the secret deal by which
United States missiles were removed from Turkey.) As the crisis
drew to an end, national security analyst Raymond Garthoff said,
"Our position on Berlin should be greatly strengthened. Our reso-
lute willingness to act in Cuba should result in a complete reas-
sessment by the Soviets as to how far they can safely push U.S. will
in general, including Berlin. Similarly it should provide our Allies
with fortitude for meeting Soviet threats."[8]

Much deserved credit has been given to members of the ExComm
during the crisis. Interestingly, none of them (except General Maxwell Taylor, of course) were military strategists. Most came from
university backgrounds; others were long-time government officials. As a group they were bright, opinionated, and inquisitive.
Their deliberations allowed for a free flow of opinion that helped
the president sort out his options. In the end, however, it was the

president alone who made the key decisions, even ignoring his Ex-Comm to conduct secret, behind-the-scenes negotiations with the Soviets. Khrushchev, on the other hand, as a product of a totalitarian society, relied on his own cunning and limited experiences. He was not, as an aide later said, "drawn to talent."[9]

President John F. Kennedy, in his 1963 American University speech, placed the dangers of nuclear confrontation in perspective when he said, ". . . nuclear powers must avert those confrontations which bring an adversary to the choice of either a humiliating retreat or a nuclear war."

Thirty years later, in 1993, the United States and Russia signed a far-reaching Strategic Arms Reduction Treaty (START II), which dramatically curtailed nuclear warheads and missiles on both sides. In a toast to Russian president Boris Yeltsin, United States president George Bush said, "The two powers that once divided the world have now come together to make it a better and safer place." As if to indicate how far the world had come since the Cuban Missile Crisis, a missile factory in the Ukraine that Nikita Khrushchev once boasted "could produce rockets like sausages" was building sausage-making machines in 1993.

Office of the Attorney General
Washington, D.C.

October 30, 1962

MEMORANDUM FOR THE SECRETARY OF STATE

FROM THE ATTORNEY GENERAL

At the request of Secretary Rusk, I telephoned Ambassador Dobrynin at approximately 7:15 p.m. on Saturday, October 27th. I asked him if he would come to the Justice Department at a quarter of eight.

We met in my office. I told him first that we understood that the work was continuing on the Soviet missile bases in Cuba. Further, I explained to him that in the last two hours we had found that our planes flying over Cuba had been fired upon and that one of our U-2's had been shot down and the pilot killed. I said these men were flying unarmed planes.

I told him that this was an extremely serious turn in events. We would have to make certain decisions within the next 12 or possibly 24 hours. There was a very little time left. If the Cubans were shooting at our planes, then we were going to shoot back. This could not help but bring on further incidents and that he had better understand the full implications of this matter.

T O P S E C R E T

Memorandum for
The Secretary of State   October 30, 1962

        He raised the point that the argument the Cubans were

making was that we were violating Cuban air space. I replied that

if we had not been violating Cuban air space then we would still be

believing what he and Khrushchev had said ▮▮▮▮ -- that there

were no long-range missiles in Cuba. In any case I said that this

matter was far more serious than the air space over Cuba and

involved peoples all over the world.

        I said that he had better understand the situation and he

had better communicate that understanding to Mr. Khrushchev.

Mr. Khrushchev and he had misled us. The Soviet Union had

secretly established missile bases in Cuba while at the same time

proclaiming, privately and publicly, that this would never be done.

I said those missile bases had to go and they had to go right away.

We had to have a commitment by at least tomorrow that those

bases would be removed. This was not an ultimatum, I said, but

just a statement of fact. He should understand that if they did not

remove those bases then we would remove them. His country

might take retaliatory action but he should understand that before

this was over, while there might be dead Americans there would

also be dead Russians.

Memorandum for
The Secretary of State   October 30, 1962

He asked me then what offer we were making. I said a
letter had just been transmitted to the Soviet Embassy which stated
in substance that the missile bases should be dismantled and all
offensive weapons should be removed from Cuba. In return, if
Cuba and Castro and the Communists ended their subversive
activities in other Central and Latin-American countries, we would
agree to keep peace in the Caribbean and not permit an invasion
from American soil.

He then asked me about Khrushchev's other proposal dealing with the removal of the missiles from Turkey. I replied that
there could be no quid pro quo -- no deal of this kind could be made.
This was a matter that had to be considered by NATO and that it
was up to NATO to make the decision. I said it was completely
impossible for NATO to take such a step under the present threatening position of the Soviet Union. If some time elapsed -- and per
your instructions. I mentioned four or five months -- I said I was
sure that these matters could be resolved satisfactorily.

Per your instructions I repeated that there could be no
deal of any kind and that any steps toward easing tensions in other
parts of the world largely depended on the Soviet Union and Mr.

Memorandum for
The Secretary of State   October 30, 1962

Khrushchev taking action in Cuba and taking it immediately.

    I repeated to him that this matter could not wait and that he had better contact Mr. Khrushchev and have a commitment from him by the next day to withdraw the missile bases under United Nations supervision for otherwise, I said, there would be drastic consequences.

RFK:amn

October 24, 1962

MEMORANDUM FOR THE PRESIDENT

FROM THE ATTORNEY GENERAL

I met with Ambassador Dobrynin last evening on the third

as you suggested
floor of the Russian Embassy and/made the following points:

I told him first that I was there on my own and not on the

instructions of the President. I said that I wanted to give him some

background on the decision of the United States Government and

wanted him to know that the duplicity of the Russians had been a

major contributing factor. When I had met with him some six weeks

before, I said, he had told me that the Russians had not placed any

long-range missiles in Cuba and had no intention to do so in the

future. He interrupted at that point and confirmed this statement

and said he specifically told me they would not put missiles in Cuba

which would be able to reach the continental United States.

I said based on that statement which I had related to the

President plus independent intelligence information at that time,

the President had gone to the American people and assured them

that the weapons being furnished by the Communists to Cuba were

defensive and that it was not necessary for the United States to blockade
or take any military action. I pointed out that this assurance of
Dobrynin to me had been confirmed by the TASS statement and then
finally, in substance, by Gromyko when he visited the President on
Thursday. I said that based on these assurances the President had
taken a different and far less belligerent position than people like
Senators Keating and Capehart, and he had assured the American
people that there was nothing to be concerned about.

I pointed out, in addition, that the President felt he had a
very helpful personal relationship with Mr. Khrushchev. Obviously,
they did not agree on many issues, but he did feel that there was a
mutual trust and confidence between them on which he could rely.
As an example of this statement I related the time that Mr. Khrushchev
requested the President to withdraw the troops from Thailand and
that step was taken within 24 hours.

I said that with the background of this relationship, plus the
specific assurances that had been given to us, and then the statement
of Dobrynin from Khrushchev to Ted Sorensen and to me that no
incident would occur before the American elections were completed,

Memorandum for The President
Page Three   October 24, 1962

we felt the action by Khrushchev and the Russians at this time was

hypocritical, misleading and false. I said this should be clearly

understood by them as it was by us.

Dobrynin's only answer was that he had told me no missiles

were in Cuba but that Khrushchev had also given similar assurances

through TASS and as far as he (Dobrynin) knew, there were still no

missiles in Cuba.

Dobrynin in the course of the conversation made several

other points. The one he stressed was why the President did not

tell Gromyko the facts on Thursday. He said this was something

they could not understand and that if we had the information at that

time why didn't we tell Gromyko.

I answered this by making two points:

Number one, there wasn't anything the President could tell

Gromyko that Gromyko didn't know already and after all, why didn't

Gromyko tell the President this instead of, in fact, denying it. I

said in addition the President was so shocked at Gromyko's presenta-

tion and his failure to recite these facts that he felt that any effort to

have an intelligent and honest conversation would not be profitable.

Memorandum for The President
Page Four   October 24, 1962

Dobrynin went on to say that from his conversations with Gromyko he doesn't believe Gromyko thought there were any missiles in Cuba. He said he was going to contact his government to find out about this matter.

I expressed surprise that after all that had appeared in the papers, and the President's speech, that he had not had a communication on that question already.

Dobrynin seemed extremely concerned. When I left I asked him if ships were going to go through to Cuba. He replied that was their instructions last month and he assumed they had the same instructions at the present time. He also made the point that although we might have pictures, all we really knew about were the sites and not missiles and that there was a lot of difference between sites and the actual missile itself. I said I did not have to argue the point -- there were missiles in Cuba -- we knew that they were there and that I hoped he would inform himself also.

I left around 10:15 p.m. and went to the White House and gave a verbal report to the President.

RFK:amn
cc/Secretary Rusk

NOTES

1. The original NATO members were Belgium, Canada, Denmark, France, Great Britain, Iceland, Italy, Luxembourg, Netherlands, Norway, Portugal, and the United States. Greece and Turkey became members in 1952 and West Germany joined in 1955.

2. No event has received as much credit for ending McCarthy's career as the March 9, 1954, *See It Now* television program on CBS. In a half-hour program, legendary broadcaster Edward R. Murrow told McCarthy's story, using the senator's own words.

3. Finkelstein, Norman H., *The Emperor General, A Biography of Douglas MacArthur* (New York: Dillon, 1989), p. 110.

4. Because of Soviet successes in launching powerful missiles into space, some in the West began to speak of a "missile gap" in the Soviet Union's favor. Indeed, the missile gap became an important issue in the 1960 presidential campaign. Only after Kennedy became president was it revealed that there really was no gap.

5. Kennedy, John F., *Strategy of Peace* (New York: Harper, 1960), p. 37.

CHAPTER TWO
AND IN THIS CORNER

1. Medvedev, Roy, *Khrushchev, A Biography* (Garden City: Doubleday, 1983), p. 87.

2. Ibid., p. 96.

3. Named after the presidential retreat in the Maryland mountains where the meeting took place. The camp was named after the grandson of President Eisenhower.

4. Kennedy, John F., *Strategy of Peace*, p. 9.

5. The U-2, a radically different airplane, was developed in the 1950s in utmost secrecy. Because of its broad wingspan and powerful engines, it was capable of flying at a maximum altitude of 75,000 feet. It was equipped with sophisticated electronic equipment and cameras.

6. In the 1960 census the Hispanic population of Dade County, Florida, which includes Miami, was 50,000. By the end of 1962 Cuban exiles had raised that number to over 200,000. *The Miami Herald*, October 18, 1992, p. 1A.

7. Beschloss, Michael, *The Crisis Years* (New York: HarperCollins, 1991), p. 114.

8. Chang, Laurence, and Peter Kornbluh, eds., *The Cuban Missile Crisis, 1962* (National Security Archives, New York: The New Press, 1992), p. 12.

9. Burlatsky, Fedor, *Khrushchev and The First Russian Spring* (New York: Scribners, 1991), p. 164.

10. Sidey, Hugh, *John F. Kennedy, President* (New York: Atheneum, 1963), p. 242.

11. National Security Archives, *The Cuban Missile Crisis, 1962*, p. 5.

12. Ibid., p. 12.

13. Gromyko, Andrei, "The Caribbean Crisis: On Glasnost Now and Secrecy Then." Originally published in *Izvestia*, April 15, 1989,

and translated into English in *The Current Digest of the Soviet Press*, vol. 4, no. 15, May 17, 1989.

CHAPTER THREE
THE BUILDUP

1. Between September and November 1961 the Soviet Union tested over thirty different nuclear weapons. Concern about the worldwide spread of radioactivity from testing on both sides was intense.

2. *The New York Times*, April 19, 1961.

3. *The Miami Herald*, April 17, 1983, p. 3.

4. Sidey, Hugh, *John F. Kennedy, President*, p. 140.

5. National Security Archives, *The Cuban Missile Crisis, 1962*, p. 16.

6. Ibid., p. 23.

7. From the United States Congressional Record of August 31, 1962, p. 18360.

8. Memorandum from Arthur Schlesinger, Jr., to McGeorge Bundy, August 22, 1962, John F. Kennedy Library.

0. CIA Intelligence Memorandum, John F. Kennedy Library, October 22, 1962.

10. *The New York Times*, September 5, 1962.

11. Beschloss, Michael, *The Crisis Years*, p. 420.

12. Sorensen, Theodore, *Kennedy* (New York: Harper, 1965), p. 667.

13. Missiles are designed for different delivery options. Ground-to-ground missiles carry payloads from a land-based site in one country to a target in another. Surface-to-air missiles are also land-based but are used to target planes in the air.

14. Medvedev, Roy, *Khrushchev, A Biography*, p. 187.

CHAPTER FOUR
PICTURES DON'T LIE

1. Surface-to-air missiles are defensive in nature, with a limited range of less than fifty miles. They are used to intercept and destroy enemy aircraft.

2. CIA Intelligence Memorandum, John F. Kennedy Library, August 22, 1962.

3. Actually, at the height of the crisis more than forty thousand Soviet troops were on the island. United Press International report, January 11, 1989.

4. CIA Intelligence Memorandum, John F. Kennedy Library, August 22, 1962.

5. Department of State Memorandum, John F. Kennedy Library, September 5, 1962.

6. Memorandum from Arthur Schlesinger, Jr., to McGeorge Bundy, John F. Kennedy Library, August 22, 1962.

7. In 1993 the CIA admitted that intelligence analysts in Washington in 1962 discounted most of these reports, believing the Soviet buildup in Cuba was defensive. One such discounted report was from an informer who described driving out of Havana and seeing "what looked like huge tubes extending over the entire length of the flatbed and completely covered with canvas." *The Boston Globe*, October 20, 1993, p. 6.

8. By 1962 the IL-28 bombers were already considered obsolete. Nonetheless, they were still capable of flying nuclear bombs from Havana to points within the United States.

9. The Soviet SS-4 MRBM had a range of approximately eleven hundred miles, capable of reaching targets in a good part of the United States.

10. Brugioni, Dino, *Eyeball to Eyeball* (New York: Random House, 1991), p. 202.

CHAPTER FIVE
DANGEROUS DECEPTION

1. Brugioni, Dino, *Eyeball to Eyeball*, p. 219.

2. Abel, Elie, *The Missile Crisis* (Philadelphia: Lippincott, 1966), p. 32.

3. Memorandum of Theodore Sorensen, John F. Kennedy Library, October 17, 1962.

4. Abel, *The Missile Crisis*, pp. 36–37.

5. Ibid., pp. 48–50.

6. Kennedy, Robert, *Thirteen Days* (New York: Norton, 1969), p. 31.

7. Transcript of ExComm Meeting Number 1, October 16, 1962. John F. Kennedy Library.

8. Transcript of ExComm Meeting Number 2, October 16, 1962. John F. Kennedy Library.

9. Bundy, McGeorge, *Danger and Survival* (New York: Random House, 1988), p. 398.

10. Transcript of second ExComm Meeting, October 16, 1962. John F. Kennedy Library.

11. Kennedy, *Thirteen Days*, p. 27.

12. Abel, Elie, *The Missile Crisis*, p. 62.

13. Memorandum of Theodore Sorensen, John F. Kennedy Library, October 20, 1962.

CHAPTER SIX
BLOCKADE

1. Sorensen, Theodore, *Kennedy*, p. 694.

2. The National Security Council was established by Congress in 1947 to advise the president on defense matters.

3. Oral History Interview of Dean Acheson, 1964. John F. Kennedy Library.

4. Garthoff, Raymond, *Reflections on the Cuban Missile Crisis* (Washington: Brookings Institution, 1989), p. 64.

5. Brugioni, Dino, *Eyeball to Eyeball*, p. 360.

6. National Security Archives, *The Cuban Missile Crisis, 1962*, pp. 146–147.

7. Ibid., pp. 148–149.

8. Abel, Elie, *The Missile Crisis*, p. 104.

9. Archives, *The Cuban Missile Crisis, 1962*, pp. 150–154.

10. Kennedy, Robert F., *Thirteen Days*, pp. 36–37.

11. Thant, U. *View from the UN* (Garden City: Doubleday, 1978), pp, 156–157.

12. Kondrashov, Stanislav, "Once More About the Caribbean Crisis," in *Izvestia*, February 28, 1989, as translated in *The Current Digest of the Soviet Press*, February 29, 1989, vol 41, no. 9.

13. Archives, *The Cuban Missile Crisis, 1962*, p. 156.

14. Beschloss, Michael, *The Crisis Years*, p. 488.

15. Archives, *The Cuban Missile Crisis, 1962*, pp. 161–162.

16. Allyn, Bruce, James Blight, and David Welch, eds., *Back to the Brink, Proceedings of the Moscow Conference on the Cuban Missile Crisis, January 27–28, 1989* (Cambridge: Harvard University Press, 1992), p. 86.

CHAPTER SEVEN
ON THE BRINK

1. Brugioni, Dino, *Eyeball to Eyeball*, p. 322.

2. *The Miami Herald*, October 24, 1962, p. 1.

3. Kennedy, Robert F., *Thirteen Days*, p. 68.

4. Ibid., p. 70.

5. Ibid.

6. National Security Archives, *The Cuban Missile Crisis, 1962*, p. 370.

7. Ibid., *The Cuban Missile Crisis, 1962*, pp. 163–164.

8. Ibid., p. 173.

9. Lippmann, Walter, "Today and Tomorrow," *The Washington Post*, October 25, 1962.

10. Archives, *The Cuban Missile Crisis, 1962*, p. 174.

CHAPTER EIGHT
DIPLOMATIC OFFENSIVE

1. Khrushchev, Nikita, *Khrushchev Remembers, The Glasnost Tapes* (Boston: Little, Brown, 1990), p. 177.

2. Summary Record, National Security Council ExComm Meeting Number 6, October 26, 1962, John F. Kennedy Library.

3. Draft telegram, John F. Kennedy Library.

4. Memorandum from Presidential Naval Aide to Evelyn Lincoln, October 26, 1962, John F. Kennedy Library.

5. A copy of the hastily typed note is reproduced in the National Security Archive's *The Cuban Missile Crisis, 1962*, p. 184.

6. Abel, Elie, *The Missile Crisis*, p. 157.

7. National Security Archives, *The Cuban Missile Crisis, 1962*, pp. 186–188.

8. Beschloss, Michael, *The Crisis Years*, p. 523.

CHAPTER NINE
BLACK SATURDAY

1. Newhouse, John, *War and Peace in the Nuclear Age* (New York: Knopf, 1989), p. 178.

2. National Security Archives, *The Cuban Missile Crisis, 1962*, p. 212.

3. Transcript of ExComm Meeting, October 27, 1962, John F. Kennedy Library.

4. Memorandum of ExComm Meeting Number 8, October 27, 1962, John F. Kennedy Library.

5. Memorandum of Roger Hilsman, State Department, October 27, 1962, John F. Kennedy Library.

6. Bundy, McGeorge, *Danger and Survival*, pp. 438–439.

7. Archives, *The Cuban Missile Crisis, 1962*, pp. 223–225.

8. Kennedy, Robert F., *Thirteen Days*, p. 107.

9. Memorandum, October 30, 1962, John F. Kennedy Library.

10. Kennedy, *Thirteen Days*, p. 109.

11. Memorandum, October 30, 1962, John F. Kennedy Library.

12. Kennedy, *Thirteen Days*, pp. 108–109.

13. Transcript of ExComm Meeting, October 27, 1962, John F. Kennedy Library.

14. As reported by United Press International, January 11, 1989.

15. Record of ExComm Meeting Number 10, October 28, 1962, John F. Kennedy Library.

CHAPTER TEN
STEPPING BACK FROM DANGER

1. Abel, Elie, *The Missile Crisis*, pp. 191–193.

2. Khrushchev, Nikita, *Khrushchev Remembers, The Glasnost Tapes*, p. 178.

3. Ibid., p. 182.

4. Sorensen, Theodore, *The Kennedy Legacy* (New York: Macmillan, 1969), p. 188.

5. Blight, James, and Donald Welch, *On the Brink*, p. 63.

6. Newhouse, John, *War and Peace in the Nuclear Age*, p. 169.

7. Sorensen, *The Kennedy Legacy*, p. 193.

8. Memorandum, October 29, 1962, John F. Kennedy Library.

9. Burlatsky, Fedor, *Khrushchev and the First Russian Spring*, p. 183.

TIMELINE OF EVENTS

THE CUBAN MISSILE CRISIS

BEFORE

January 1, 1959	Fidel Castro assumes power in Cuba.
August 28, 1960	United States places embargo on trade with Cuba.
December 19, 1960	Cuba aligns itself with Soviet policies.
January 3, 1961	United States severs diplomatic relations with Cuba.
January 20, 1961	John F. Kennedy is inaugurated as president.
April 17–18, 1961	Bay of Pigs is invaded by Cuban exiles.
June 3–4, 1961	Summit conference between John F. Kennedy and Nikita Khrushchev is held in Vienna, Austria.
August 12, 1961	Berlin Wall erected.

Late 1961	CIA begins top-secret Operation Mongoose with the goal of toppling Castro.
January 30, 1962	Organization of American States excludes Cuba from membership.
Late April 1962	Khrushchev decides to place missiles in Cuba.
Mid-July 1962	Soviet ships begin ferrying missiles, troops, launch equipment and other military supplies to Cuba. U.S. monitors shipping activity.
August 10, 1962	John McCone, director of the Central Intelligence Agency, sends the president a memorandum indicating his belief that medium-range ballistic missiles (MRBMs) will be placed in Cuba by the Soviets.
Mid-August 1962	Reports to U.S. intelligence agencies indicate the presence of offensive missiles in Cuba. Many of the reports are proven false or linked to the buildup of SAM defensive missiles.
August 29, 1962	A U.S. U-2 reconnaissance flight over Cuba reveals the presence of SA-2 SAM sites in Cuba.
August 31, 1962	Senator Kenneth Keating reveals the presence of Soviet missiles in Cuba.
September 4, 1962	President Kennedy publicly reveals the presence of Soviet defensive missiles and troops in Cuba. He says there are no offensive missiles on the island. The Soviet ambassador assures Robert Kennedy that no offensive missiles will be placed in Cuba.
September 15, 1962	The first Soviet MRBMs arrive in Cuba.
September 20, 1962	U.S. Senate passes Resolution 230, sanctioning the use of force to curb aggression in Cuba.

September 21, 1962   Soviet foreign minister Andrei Gromyko tells the United Nations that a U.S. attack on Cuba or Cuban-bound ships would mean war.

September 1962   Rumors abound in Washington about the Soviet military buildup in Cuba. Calls for action.

October 9, 1962   The president approves a U-2 flight over Cuba. Bad weather delays the flight until October 14.

October 14, 1962   U-2 flight photographs suspected sites in western Cuba.

DURING

October 15, 1962   Analysts at the National Photographic Interpretation Center discover MRBM sites.

October 16, 1962   McGeorge Bundy informs the president of the findings. Kennedy orders assembly of trusted advisers, the ExComm. During several meetings that day, ExComm members deliberate about possible courses of action. Utmost secrecy is invoked throughout the next six days' deliberations.

October 17, 1962   Khrushchev sends a message by informal channels to Kennedy, saying that "under no circumstances would surface-to-surface missiles be sent to Cuba." ExComm debates air strike versus blockade options. New U-2 flights reveal additional MRBM sites in varying stages of construction.

October 18, 1962   Military buildup in southeastern United States takes place under cover of previously scheduled "training exercises." Soviet foreign minister Gromyko visits the president and assures him that military aid to Cuba is strictly defensive.

October 19, 1962 President Kennedy leaves for scheduled campaign trip. ExComm debate continues.

October 20, 1962 In Chicago the president develops a "slight cold" and returns to Washington in response to call that the ExComm has decided on what action to take in Cuba.

October 21, 1962 President Kennedy decides on a quarantine of Cuba as a first action to remove the offensive missiles from Cuba. There is a diplomatic flurry of activity as American allies are secretly informed.

October 22, 1962 At 7:00 P.M. (EST) President Kennedy addresses the nation and reveals the crisis and his course of action. The alert status of United States military forces is raised.

October 23, 1962 The Organization of American States unanimously endorses the U.S. action. The Soviet Union requests a meeting of the UN Security Council. President Kennedy signs official Proclamation of Interdiction, to go into effect the next day.

October 24, 1962 A number of Soviet ships reverse course before reaching the interdiction line. In Moscow, Khrushchev meets with an American businessman and sends a message through him to Kennedy. The U.S. Strategic Air Command raises its defense alert status to DEFCON 2, the highest ever. Diplomatic efforts continue at the UN.

October 25, 1962 Newspaper columnist Walter Lippmann proposes trade of Soviet missiles in Cuba for U.S. missiles in Turkey. ExComm continues to analyze the situation. Soviets con-

	tinue work on Cuban missile sites. U Thant, secretary general of the United Nations, proposes a temporary halt in the actions of both sides.
October 26, 1962	U.S. Navy boards the *Marucla*, a ship under Soviet charter. John Scali, ABC network correspondent, meets Alexander Fomin of the Soviet embassy. Fomin proposes a solution. A private letter from Khrushchev to President Kennedy proposes a peaceful solution to the crisis. ExComm prepares to respond positively. Robert Kennedy meets secretly with Soviet ambassador and suggests Cuban-Turkish missile trade.
October 27, 1962	Second Khrushchev letter arrives over a public Radio Moscow broadcast with an official proposal for a Cuban-Turkish trade. Kennedy does not tell ExComm about secret proposal, and ExComm opposes public trade. A U.S. U-2 strays over Soviet territory. A second U-2, this one over Cuba, is shot down by orders of a local Soviet commander without permission from Moscow. The American pilot is killed. The crisis deepens. U.S. air strikes at Cuba loom as next step. ExComm makes plans. An angry John Scali confronts Fomin. On his own, Scali issues warning of immediate U.S. attack. That evening Robert Kennedy again meets secretly with Dobrynin and assures him that U.S. will remove missiles from Turkey but that Turkey must not be part of any public agreement to end the crisis. He strongly warns that if the Soviets do not remove the

Cuban missiles at once, American forces "would remove them." Kennedy sends Khrushchev a message accepting the Soviet leader's October 26th proposals but publicly ignoring the Turkish aspect of the second letter.

October 28, 1962   Over Radio Moscow, Nikita Khrushchev accepts Kennedy's response. The crisis ends.

AFTER

November 1962   Negotiations continue on the details of the removal of Soviet offensive weapons from Cuba. Relations are strained between the Soviets and Cubans. By November 20 all missiles and bomber aircraft are removed. U.S. forces return to normal peacetime alert levels.

November 21, 1962   President Kennedy officially ends the quarantine.

THE MAJOR PLAYERS

Acheson, Dean Secretary of state, 1949–1953. During the Kennedy administration, he served as an unofficial adviser.

Ball, George Under secretary of state, 1962–1968.

Bundy, McGeorge Assistant to the president for national security affairs, 1961–1966. Before joining the Kennedy administration, he was dean of Harvard College, the Arts and Sciences School of Harvard University.

Castro, Fidel Communist prime minister of Cuba since his 1959 revolution seized power.

Dobrynin, Anatoly Soviet ambassador to the United States, 1962–1986.

Fomin, Alexander Officially the counselor at the Soviet embassy in Washington, he was the station chief in the United States of the KGB, the Soviet intelligence organization.

Gromyko, Andrei Foreign minister of the Soviet Union, 1957–1986.

Hilsman, Roger Assistant secretary for intelligence and research, State Department, 1961–1963.

Kennedy, John F. 35th president of the United States, 1961–1963.

Kennedy, Robert F. Attorney general of the United States, 1961–1964. Brother of the president.

Khrushchev, Nikita Premier of the Soviet Union, 1958–1964.

Lansdale, Edward Chief of Operation Mongoose, a secret program to oust Fidel Castro and the Communist government of Cuba, 1961–1962.

Lundhal, Arthur Chief, National Photographic Interpretation Center in Washington, D.C.

Martin, Edwin Assistant secretary of state for Inter-American Affairs, 1962–1964.

McCone, John Director, Central Intelligence Agency, 1961–1965.

McNamara, Robert Secretary of defense, 1961–1968. Former president of the Ford Motor Company.

Rostow, Walt Whitman Director of policy planning, State Department, 1961–1966.

Rusk, Dean Secretary of state, 1961–1969.

Scali, John Washington-based diplomatic correspondent, ABC News, 1961–1971.

Schlesinger, Arthur M. Special assistant to the president, 1961–1964. A noted historian and author.

Sorensen, Theodore Special counsel to the president. He was John Kennedy's main speechwriter and adviser.

Stevenson, Adlai   United States ambassador to the United Nations, 1961–1965. Democratic candidate for president in 1952 and 1956.

Taylor, General Maxwell   Military adviser to the president, 1961–1962. Chairman of the Joint Chiefs of Staff, October 1962 to July 1964.

Thant, U   Acting secretary general of the United Nations, 1961–1962; secretary general, 1962–1971.

FURTHER READING

Abel, Elie. *The Missile Crisis*. Philadelphia: Lippincott, 1966.

Allyn, Bruce, James Blight, and David Welch, eds. *Back to the Brink, Proceedings of the Moscow Conference on the Cuban Missile Crisis, January 27–28, 1989*. Cambridge: Harvard University Press, 1992.

Beschloss, Michael. *The Crisis Years*. New York: HarperCollins, 1991.

Blight, James, and David Welch. *On the Brink*. New York: Farrar, Straus and Giroux, 1989.

Brugioni, Dino. *Eyeball to Eyeball*. New York: Random House, 1991.

Bundy, McGeorge. *Danger and Survival*. New York: Random House, 1988.

Burlatsky, Fedor. *Khrushchev, The First Russian Spring*. New York: Scribners, 1991.

Chang, Laurence, and Peter Kornbluh, eds. *The Cuban Missile Crisis, 1962* (National Security Archive). New York: The New Press, 1992.

Garthoff, Raymond. *Reflections on the Cuban Missile Crisis.* Washington: Brookings Institution, 1989.

Gromyko, Andrei. *Memoirs.* New York: Doubleday, 1989.

Kennedy, John F. *The Strategy of Peace.* New York: Harper, 1960.

Kennedy, Robert F. *Thirteen Days.* New York: Norton, 1969.

Khrushchev, Nikita. *Khrushchev Remembers, The Glasnost Tapes.* Boston: Little, Brown, 1990.

Khrushchev, Sergei. *Khrushchev on Khrushchev.* Boston: Little, Brown, 1990.

Kort, Michael. *Nikita Khrushchev.* New York: Watts, 1989.

Medvedev, Roy. *Khrushchev, A Biography.* Garden City: Doubleday, 1983.

Newhouse, John. *War and Peace in the Nuclear Age.* New York: Knopf, 1989.

Schlesinger, Arthur M. *A Thousand Days.* Boston: Houghton-Mifflin, 1965.

Sidey, Hugh. *John F. Kennedy, President.* New York: Atheneum, 1963.

Sorensen, Theodore. *Kennedy.* New York: Harper, 1965.

Sorensen, Theodore. *The Kennedy Legacy.* New York: Macmillan, 1969.

Thant, U. *View from the UN.* Garden City: Doubleday, 1978.

Thompson, Robert Smith. *The Missiles of October.* New York: Simon & Schuster, 1992.

INDEX